CW01648372

ANDREW WEIGHT grew up in Hastings on the East Sussex coast. After graduating from Reading University with a degree in Sociology, he worked in the finance industry in London and Geneva, latterly as a founding partner of an award-winning wealth management business. He left this business and moved to the Swiss countryside in 2009. He has now returned to his roots in East Sussex, where he writes, advises small businesses and start-ups and buys and sells classic motorcycles.

ARTFULNESS OR DECEIT?

ANDREW WEIGHT

RGP

RAKE GALLANT PUBLISHING
Rye

First published in 2024 by
Rake Gallant Publishing
Doucegrove Farm
Doucegrove Lane
Northiam
Rye
East Sussex TN31 6JQ

A catalogue record for this book is available from the British Library.

PAPERBACK ISBN 978-0-9927568-4-0
eISBN 978-0-9927568-5-7

Typeset by Octavo Smith Publishing Services

To Della, Helen and Louise
for their unconditional support
and encouragement.

ARTFULNESS

SEPTEMBER 1997

'So, do you feel guilty afterwards?'

Sophie turned on to her side and lay looking at Henri. She felt quite comfortable naked next to him; there had been a time when she would not have done.

'No, not really. Something died between Johnny and me that day.' She shivered a little as she thought about it.

'How has my old friend been?'

'He seems fine. You'll see for yourself later.'

'Well, as you know I haven't seen him since that last New Year we all came to Sussex.'

'I do, yes. It's only a couple of years but seems like so much longer. I don't suppose it's anything to do with the fact that you've been screwing his wife in the meantime?' Sophie was surprised how excited saying it out loud made her feel.

'Anyway, I didn't ask about you. Does it make you feel guilty?'

'If my friend Johnny is stupid enough to neglect his beautiful wife, why should I feel guilty?'

He kissed her mouth lightly. She watched as he walked over to the window of the hotel room and stood looking out over the Thames. His back was lightly muscled, and his buttocks were small and firm. As he strode about the room there was no doubt that Henri felt comfortable naked in front of her. Their covert meetings had been few and far between since that New Year's Day in 1995, only a handful before today. She could remember them all quite clearly; three times in Paris, when she had been to see Juste and Véronique to buy clothes for her vintage-clothes shop in Rye High Street, then twice in London when Henri had come over on business. Five meetings, five hotel rooms, five afternoons, evenings and nights of very enjoyable but rather loveless sex. She watched as he tapped a cigarette out of his packet of Disque Bleu on to the bedside table, lit it and then inhaled the smoke deeply before exhaling, his narrow but well-toned chest rising and falling with the action. It still felt dangerous – the deceit, the sex, Henri – that's why she did it. And a little part of her did it because of what she had seen Johnny doing with Mark. They were all meeting up later at the *Sensation* exhibition. Johnny was desperate for them all to meet his new friend Arthur Swale who was an exhibitor.

'We have to go soon,' she said to Henri.

'*Oui, mon amour*, but not together. I'll leave a few minutes before you.'

The deception was implicit in all they did together.

***

'It doesn't seem to bother you these days.' said Mark.

'No, it doesn't.'

Mark and Johnny had just sat back down in the Compton Arms after a brief intimate skirmish in the pub toilets. The bar was quite busy with the early-evening office crowd, so Mark hoped that their ten minutes in the gents had gone unnoticed by their fellow drinkers. He still loved surprising Johnny with a quick handjob, the danger of doing it in public adding to the thrill.

'Why do you think that is?'

'Dunno, mate. Familiarity maybe? I've known you longer than Sophie.'

They still had to be careful not to let Sophie find out how frequently they saw one another. Since that fateful day when she had caught them in flagrante, Mark had seen little of his old university friend Sophie. His schoolmate Johnny had insisted they keep quiet about the bulk of their reunions, whether they just be a quick drink, a lovers' tryst or both. Generally, Johnny let him know when he was in London, and Mark made sure he was available to meet him.

'I'm quite looking forward to seeing Sophie tonight. You were the one that messed our friendship up.' Mark smiled at Johnny.

'You were getting nowhere fast, pal.'

Mark was happy to let Johnny continue bragging like this. His college crush on Sophie, he now realised, had been no more than that. He really did wish they could recapture their old friendship but knew that it was pretty unlikely. Too much water had passed under various bridges. Johnny was more important in any case. He deliberately changed the subject.

'So, what time do we need to arrive at the Royal Academy? I'm not quite sure how you managed to wangle four tickets. According to the papers, they're like gold dust.'

'All those hours I've put in at the Groucho seem to have finally paid a dividend. Arthur was helpful, too. Even the artists only get one ticket each, you know.'

'Really? You *have* done well to get us all into the private view then. Tell me more about Arthur Swale.'

'He's a northern bigot. From Scunthorpe. We seem to get along for some reason. I'm a southern bigot, so I suppose that must help.'

Mark watched as Johnny pulled on his Marlboro Light with a smirk. His cheek bones were still well defined, but the booze and fags were starting to take their toll on his skin.

'Jack Daniels might be another common interest, I'm guessing.'

'Correct.'

'Well, I look forward to meeting him. His stuff doesn't seem to have created as much fuss as that picture of Myra Hindley.'

'No. That's by a guy called Marcus Harvey, who I think I've met somewhere or other. What do you think of it?'

'I think it's offensive.'

'Really? I think it's provocative but not offensive.'

'Unless you're the parents of one of those kids that she killed.' Mark was quite firm in his view on this.

'You may have a point. You remember Jake Chapman from school?'

'I think he was in the year above us.'

'Exactly. He and his brother Dinos are in the show, too.'

'They've done well then.'

'Too fucking right. This thing's going to be massive you know. The YBAs they're calling them, the Young British Artists. These guys are the new rock stars.'

'Well, I suppose it would take one to recognise that.'

Mark watched Johnny smile at the compliment. His career had not quite worked out since he left Swerve, but Mark did his best to prop up Johnny's ego.

'Where are you meeting Sophie?'

'We said that we'd meet outside. She's got the tickets.'

'What about Henri?'

'Outside, too. It'll be good to see the old scoundrel again.'

'That's the old scoundrel who slept with your wife.'

'Yeah, I know. Seems she still sees him occasionally when she goes to Paris. It doesn't bother me. I never held it against him for some reason. It must be his Gallic charm.'

'If you say so.' Mark, however, had not forgiven Henri for the Paisley Records débâcle and the damage it had done to his professional reputation. The bankruptcy of Johnny's old record company, and the subsequent disappearance of Charles Cooper-Smythe, its founder, had forced Mark out of his old job. It had turned out for the better, however, as he was much happier where he was now.

***

The taxi drove down Piccadilly towards the Royal Academy. Sophie only came up to London a few times a year these days but always enjoyed it when she did. Today's liaison with Henri seemed to have honed all her senses; she felt receptive and eager to see the art. She was wearing a short, black, shoulderless dress with a denim jacket over it; she hoped it was the right mixture of chic and cool. She was also wearing her current favourite shade of red Rimmel lipstick, which lately seemed to enhance her confidence. She was still a little apprehensive about seeing Mark, and although sleeping with Henri had allowed the apprehension to recede somewhat, the antipathy was still there. It had been nearly five years since she had accidentally and covertly witnessed him sucking her husband's cock in her own living-room. Unsurprisingly, she and Johnny had subsequently been estranged for a while after the whole thing had become public on that fateful night in Lausanne, when Mark had outed her affair with Henri, and Henri, in turn, had taken his revenge by letting Johnny and Mark know that Sophie had seen them in flagrante. But she and Johnny had made a go of it again, as much for the sake of Amy as anything. Amy, the reason they were together in the first place. Seven and a half now and bright as a button. Sophie was pretty sure that Johnny still saw Mark in London more often than he let on, but she wasn't sure if there was still anything physical between them. It was not a subject she chose to dwell on these days. The music scene that Johnny was involved in was in London, he had to be there regularly, and she had given up worrying about whom he saw and what he did when he was there.

The taxi pulled up outside the Royal Academy, and she saw the three men of the moment waiting for her on the pavement: Johnny, Henri and Mark. She was inextricably linked to them. Johnny looking handsomely gaunt in his Armani sunglasses, Henri in a well-cut dark-blue suit, suave but conservative, and Mark looking as if he was ready for a night in the pub, in his slightly laddish, untucked button-down shirt.

She decided to kiss Mark on both cheeks and at least outwardly pretend they had buried the hatchet. He was more than civil, too, and managed to greet her warmly. Henri then expressed his delight in seeing her for the first time in ages. She winced inwardly at his pretence. Apparently, a perfect gentleman. She knew better. She linked arms with Johnny as they followed the crowd through to the gallery.

As they went through she took in the other guests. It was a real mix of people: those who looked to be the great and the good of the Royal Academy, well-heeled and conservatively dressed, grey-haired men in suits, older women in cocktail dresses; there were also older creative types, artists she guessed, dressed in eccentricities and conceits, lots of headwear and scarves, sculpted facial hair for the men and bright make-up and big jewellery for the women; then there were a smaller number of younger people, in their late twenties and thirties, whom Sophie recognised as some of the artists accompanied by hangers on. They were scruffier, livelier, laughing, necking the free booze, some dressed up but inexpensively. There was an androgyny to the clothes they wore: jeans, T-shirts, maybe a jacket. They stood around in groups, obviously well acquainted; this was their crowd. Sophie knew some of their names: Damien Hirst, Tracey Emin. She had heard Johnny talking about having been at school with the Chapman Brothers, but she hadn't met them before. Recently he had talked a lot about Arthur Swale, whom he had met at the Groucho Club in Soho. Johnny's trips to London tended to be work related but often ended in drinking sessions. Swerve, despite its demise, still gave him enough minor-celebrity status to meet someone like Arthur. At least this had resulted in the tickets for tonight.

'Arthur, you twat,' Johnny yelled. He had obviously spotted Arthur Swale.

'Fuck off, you loser.' Arthur, it seemed had an equally bluff delivery. He had a broad accent that Sophie recognised as being generally northern rather than anything more specific. He stood a few yards from them in a gaggle of what looked like other artists. He was a big man with wild, dark hair, worn quite long, and a wide ruddy face. He was wearing a battered parka, turned-up jeans and steel toe cap boots. He had an aura of debauched charisma. He engulfed Johnny's slight physique in a bear hug.

'This is Sophie,' said Johnny.

'A pleasure to meet you,' Arthur said, taking her hand and kissing it.

'You, too, Arthur. Johnny's told me a lot about you, but I can't place your accent. Where is that from?'

'They said you couldn't take the cunt out of Scunthorpe, but here I am in London,' said Arthur.

The group around them laughed, as Arthur grinned widely at his gag. Sophie didn't approve of use of the C-word as a rule, but once she had worked out the joke she smiled. Stood next to Arthur were two tall guys with cropped hair and T-shirts.

'That's not the first time you've used that line, Arthur, is it?' the younger, taller one said.

'And it won't be the last,' Arthur rejoined. 'Scunthorpe and proud. That's me.'

'Hi, Jake,' said Johnny to the taller of the two cropped-haired guys. So these were the Chapman Brothers, thought Sophie. Jake and Dinos. They both wore band T-shirts and jeans: Funkadelic for Dinos and the Chemical Brothers for Jake.

'Sorry, do we know each other?' asked Jake.

'We were at school together, Hastings Grammar. I was in the year below, so was Mark. I'm Johnny Jones.'

'Of course, Johnny Jones of Swerve fame,' said Jake. 'Good to see you.'

Introductions were made all round, and drinks were grabbed from passing trays. It turned out that the woman in the group was Tracey Emin. Sophie suddenly wished that she had done more research before coming; as she spoke to Tracey she realised that she had no idea what she was exhibiting. They chatted away. Tracey had grown up in Margate, along the coast from Sophie's hometown of Rye, so they had plenty in common. Sophie found her spiky but engaging. She was striking looking, not beautiful, but attractive, with a friendly smile and sculpted bone structure.

Arthur's dulcet tones interrupted. 'It's time my new friends saw my exhibit. Come on, gang.'

Sophie, Johnny, Mark and Henri dutifully followed Arthur, who forged a path through the crowd. Tracey waved them goodbye, smiling her lopsided smile. Jake and Dinos looked on, smiling thinner, less genuine smiles, more the equivalent of ironically raised eyebrows. Sophie had the impression that Arthur might be a little loud and brash for them perhaps. They came over as more cerebral. As their group moved through the crowd Sophie started to take in some of the artworks in the larger rooms. Damien Hirst's shark in formaldehyde she had read about and now saw for the first time. The large cabinet filled with a preserved shark carcass loomed at her rather as she moved past. Beyond it lay the much publicised and talked about portrait of Moors Murderer Myra Hindley, large and foreboding, a blown-up version of the photographic image that had acted as a deterrent to all kids born in the sixties and seventies, a warning never talk to strangers. The photo of Hindley had frequently appeared on TV and in newspapers throughout Sophie's lifetime, often in recent years when parole for Hindley was discussed. This exhibit she knew more about as it had been all over the media before the show. Apparently, it had been recreated at scale using tiny prints of children's hands. It certainly stood out, large and provocative. She had read that the artist Marcus Harvey had described Hindley in the image as a 'misfired Marilyn Monroe'. This seemed a little glib and had certainly wound up the British tabloids. There had been a debate at the Royal Academy as to whether the work should be shown at all. The argument against being that it meant that the feelings of the surviving parents of the five children whom Hindley and Ian Brady had murdered then buried on the moors outside Manchester should be protected; the argument for being that the media had already turned the photographic image into something more than just a photograph of Myra Hindley. Typically, and duplicitously, Sophie thought, the *Sun* newspaper had championed the cause of the parents of the murdered children, despite themselves sensationalising Hindley and the image for decades. Apparently, under pressure from the ensuing scandal, the vote at the Academy had been close but came down on the side of allowing the work to be shown. She felt a strong sense of the artist's unease as she walked towards the image.

Arthur chuntered away at the head of their group. 'Hi, Damien.' He waved to Damien Hirst drinking with another group near the Hindley. 'Damien, of course, has multiple exhibits here, but I only have one. Still, better than none. Turn right, guys, and here he is.'

In the centre of a smaller room was a metal sculpture of a naked man, balanced on his shoulders and neck with his back and legs raised towards the ceiling. The result of this posture was that gravity left his penis dangling vertically downwards, pointing at his open mouth. A yellow liquid was flowing constantly from the penis into the open mouth. He was drinking his own urine.

'Meet *The Narcissist*, subtitled *Techniques in How to Be Self-Absorbed*. What do you think? I tell most people that it's my own piss circulating, but, between you and me, for practical reasons it's actually water with some yellow food colouring.'

'It's grotesque,' said Mark.

'Philistine,' said Johnny to Mark, embarrassed by his friend's outburst.

'That's a good word for it, Mark, thank you,' said Arthur without irony. He was clearly pleased that Mark found the work grotesque.

Sophie was a little lost for words. On the one hand, in the

context of the title of the work, it was witty and original. On the other hand, it was a little gross. She looked harder at the detail of the sculpture. It looked beautifully made from strips and panels of black metal riveted together. It was a kind of Meccano man pissing into his own mouth.

'It reminds me of Meccano, Arthur,' she said.

'True also,' said Arthur.

Again, she noticed that Johnny looked uncomfortable. He was looking for something more intellectual, it seemed.

'What's the message, Arthur, or are we supposed to work it out ourselves?' Johnny asked.

'The message is pretty fuckin' obvious, Johnny. The bloke's pissing in his own mouth. Make of it what you will, but the title is a bit of a giveaway.'

Johnny laughed.

'Does it represent a specific person?' Henri had been silent until now.

'It can be whoever you want it to be,' replied Arthur.

'Well, there are a number of French politicians it reminds me of,' said Henri. They all laughed. 'I think it is very powerful, Arthur.' He pronounced Arthur in the French fashion as *Artour.* Sophie had noticed how Henri sometimes did this. She wasn't sure if it was an affectation, but she found it quite cute. Henri's French accent in English was not very pronounced but detectable all the same.

'I do like it, Arthur, but I still think it's grotesque.' It was unusual for Mark to be quite this forward.

Arthur chuckled, grinning at Mark. 'I don't give a fuck whether you like it or not. I just make the stuff.'

Mark grinned back at Arthur.

Sophie was walking around the piece. It really was very well made, beautifully formed and riveted. Was the subject supposed to shock? Perhaps more shocking than the world-famous *Manneken Pis*, but, in a way, it was parodying all those cherubs peeing into fountains that were considered so endearing. There was more to Arthur underneath that bluff exterior, she thought.

'I love it, too, Arthur, but I don't love having to tell you. I can't stand looking at that self-satisfied grin for too long.' Johnny had seen enough.

'Selfish twat. You should take more pleasure in other people's success.'

'It's growing on me, Arthur,' Sophie said. 'It's probably not a drawing-room piece, but I think I like it.'

'I might be able to comment on that if I knew what a drawing-room was, love. We don't have those in Scunny.' Arthur seemed to be turning up his accent, but he was still grinning. Sophie smiled back.

She turned to Johnny. 'I'm going to have a look around. I'll find you a bit later.' She was intrigued by what the rest of the exhibition might have to offer.

She decided to seek out Tracey Emin's exhibit first and found it in a room close by. It was a blue tent, what looked like a common-or-garden tent intended for camping, one that you might buy in Millets or Blacks. Sewn around the bottom of the tent in pink capitals was the title of the work, *Everyone I Have Ever Slept with 1963–1995*. The tent was unzipped and seemed to invite the viewer inside. Sophie ducked into the small space and found a collection of names in various sizes and colours sewn on the inside. The name Billy Childish was prominent in large black capitals on a mauve-and-white floral background; there were other men's names, some large, some small, but also the names of women and some that seemed to be those of family members. Sewn into the floor was the slogan:

With myself
Always Myself
Never
Forgetting

Sophie suddenly felt very moved by the intimacy of the space. It made her think of the men she had slept with, for sure, but also the girlfriends she had grown up with, the sleepovers, the drunken teenage nights, the sleepless nights when Amy was young, the times she had climbed into her parents' bed when she was young. A flood of intimate memories overtook her, and she felt herself welling up. She was tearful but in a happy, nostalgic way. The feeling was interrupted by a well-spoken couple, dressed for a night at the Royal Opera House in Covent Garden, peering into the entrance.

'Oh, how ghastly. Don't you think, dear?' one said to the other before realising that Sophie was there. 'So sorry, we hadn't realised there was someone inside.'

They scuttled off. Sophie stepped out of the tent and took a moment to compose herself before she went off in search of the next work. She was a little shocked how the tent, despite its title, made her think of the women in her life rather than the men. She thought of her daughter Amy, her mother and, to her surprise, her friends Juste and Véronique in Paris. They were a couple, and while they weren't men haters, they certainly regarded heterosexual men with suspicion. She felt a female solidarity around them that she had also sensed from Tracey's tent. The exhibition was evoking emotion in her, inspiring her to see more. It also seemed to have brought out an urge to visit Paris again.

***

Johnny had decided to leave Arthur to a crowd of admirers who had gathered around *The Narcissist*. He wanted to seek out Sophie and spend some time looking at the art with her. Despite what he told Mark, he was always racked with guilt after one of their liaisons. Not only did he feel a little guilty for cheating on Sophie but even more so for having sex with another man. He just couldn't come to terms with it. It had never happened with anyone else. It was just easy, and Mark seemed to find him so attractive. He grabbed another glass of wine from a passing tray and drank half of it in one go. He started to look around for Sophie and was quickly stopped in his tracks. Laid out before him was a highly realistic model of a middle-aged man lying naked on his back, with his dark-ringed eyes closed, his palms by his side facing upwards, peaceful, but probably intended to look dead. He looked at the title of the work. Sure enough it was called *Dead Dad*. What made it more poignant was the fact that it was not full size; it seemed to be in proportion but only around three feet long. The nudity somehow added to the impact; the figure was vulnerable because of it, almost in the same way that a baby was. Naked when you're born, naked when you die. He thought of the void that was his own father. He had never known him. There was just a big, empty hole where he should have been. He realised that he ached to fill it. Amy should meet her grandad, too. He would have to work on his mother to let him try to find him. He couldn't bear the idea of his own father ending up like *Dead Dad* without him ever having seen him. It had always puzzled him as to why his mother, the lovely Mary, had never wanted him to know his father. He understood, now that he was older, that there must have been acute difficulties in their relationship, but were these really so extreme that he should be denied any knowledge of his own father? It had suited him to have his mother to himself when they were always together. It gave him the attention he craved. Now he no longer had that attention on a daily basis he felt a yearning for the love of his other parent. He had fantasised about his father, how he was, how he looked. He imagined a kind man, young for his age, well dressed, clever and well read. He looked back at *Dead Dad*, and that was not what he saw; he saw an old, worn-out-looking, vulnerable man, as if on a slab in the mortuary, alone. He drank the other half of his wine. He needed another drink and a cigarette. He would probably have to go outside for that. He grabbed a glass of wine as the next server passed by and headed for the exit. He really had to find his father.

***

Henri found himself left with Arthur and Mark.

'Do you think you could give us a bit of a tour, Arthur. I'd like to know what you think of some of these other pieces,' said Mark.

'Sure, I can show you around, but I'm not a tour guide. You need to form your own opinions about the art.'

'Well said, *mon ami*. I take your point. There is one thing I would appreciate, however. Would you be so kind as to introduce me to Damien Hirst, Arthur?' Something about the shark had piqued Henri's interest.

'Why do you want to talk to that dickhead when you're with me?' Arthur seemed a little disgruntled by the request. Or maybe it was his sense of humour; Henri sometimes found it difficult to interpret the British.

However, as they moved into the main gallery, Arthur called out, 'Oi, Hirst, French bloke here wants to meet you!'

Damien Hirst turned around from a group of what looked like potential investors rather than other artists. They were gathered around the shark.

Henri walked over with his arm outstretched. 'Henri le Cerf. Delighted to meet you, Damien.'

'Damien Hirst. Likewise,' said Damien. Henri had noticed immediately that he was slight in stature; he had cropped hair and an intense expression. His manner, however, was open and friendly.

'I love the shark,' Henri said. 'What is it called?'

'*The Physical Impossibility of Death in the Mind of Someone Living*,' Damien replied. 'I made it for Charles Saatchi in 1991. It's been around for a while now, and it is kind of deteriorating physically. How do you know that idiot Swale by the way?' He spoke quickly with a slight accent, similar to Arthur's but not as pronounced.

'I was just introduced to him by Johnny Jones, an old friend.'

'Johnny Jones from Swerve? Another idiot!' Damien said grinning. 'I know him from the Groucho Club. You know all the idiots it seems, Henri.'

He laughed, more as a deliberate show of appreciation for Hirst's joke than because he thought it was funny. Henri was intrigued but slightly disarmed by Hirst.

'So how did you come to create the shark?' he asked.

'Well, as I said, Charles Saatchi commissioned me to create the piece. I could choose what it was going to be, and he would fund it. It's not a cheap thing to do, so the fact that I knew we had his money behind it enabled me to crystallise an idea I had been thinking about for quite a while. Really, it's about death, I suppose. I don't think we talk about death enough. It's the one certainty in life, yet no one is taught how to prepare for it. We're taught how to live but not how to die. So, without wanting to be obvious, I think the fact that the shark is dead is a big part of it. But it's obviously also about aesthetics. If you take away the smell of the carcass with the formaldehyde, there's a beauty in the dead shark.'

'I completely agree,' said Henri. 'There is a power to the animal even in death. I have always loved sharks. They're so sleek, so intimidating, the top of the food chain.'

'I'm glad you like it. Apologies, I need to get back to the people I was talking to,' said Damien. And just like that he slipped away.

Henri didn't think about death when he looked at the shark. He saw power. And to him power meant money. This guy was on to something. The idea was simple, but so innovative. Sometimes Henri imagined himself as a shark, in business, in relationships, he wanted to dominate and succeed. This artwork inspired him to do that. He felt a familiar adrenaline rush. He needed to know more about this contemporary art scene. He could smell an opportunity, and where there was opportunity there was money to be made. He didn't want to miss out.

***

'So, what kind of art do you like, Mark?' asked Arthur.

'To be honest, I'm not really sure, Arthur. It's not something I've ever really thought about. I suppose I like traditional art.'

'What does that mean?'

'Well, I suppose paintings, things that are quite representational, logical. I'm not that keen on anything abstract really. Those paintings that are just a few coloured blocks. They're not really my thing. I do like those Warhol cans of soup, though, if we are talking about modern art. I like the symmetry. They're a bit meaningless, but I am quite drawn to the way they look.'

'Do you normally go to art galleries?'

'No, I'm afraid I don't really. I'm enjoying this, though. I'm an accountant, Arthur. I'm quite analytical. I was drawn to things like maths and economics at school. Art was always a bit of a mystery to me. Johnny and I were schoolmates; he's my window into this world. I've always been into music, though. I was a huge Swerve fan, and I'm really into what Johnny's doing now. As he said, I suppose I am a bit of a philistine when it comes to art.'

'You just haven't woken up the beast, Mark. A beast lurks in all of us. Let me show you something.'

They walked into another part of the gallery, and Arthur stopped by a collection of what looked like children's shop mannequins to Mark, only they were welded together into one continuous circle, maybe a dozen of them, their torsos fused. As Mark looked closer he became more shocked, they wore nothing but trainers and wigs, but some of them had penises as noses, and some of them anuses or vaginas as mouths, he wasn't sure which. The overall look of the dummies was strangely androgynous.

'This is *Zygotic Acceleration, biogenetic, de-sublimated libidinal model (enlarged x 1000).*' Arthur announced the title in an ironic tone. 'It's by your mates Jake and Dinos, or, to give them their working name, the Chapman Brothers. What do you reckon?'

'It's shocking,' said Mark. 'In both senses of the word: I'm shocked, and it's shockingly bad.'

'Why do you say that? Shocking I can understand as a reaction. Bad?'

'Do I have to explain, Arthur? It's perverse. Bad as in not good. Bad as in disgraceful.'

'What makes it perverse? It's only perverse if you take it seriously. I think it's funny.'

'Really? How can you laugh at it? They're children, aren't they?' Mark was quite upset.

'I'm sure it's a joke, knowing Jake and Dinos, and you've walked into the trap. They're using everyday things that you can find in any high street and making them shockingly ridiculous. It's the fact that they've put genitals on the faces of the mannequins that shocks you, but kids are sexualised in our media the whole time. That's what's truly shocking in our society. They're laughing at hypocrisy, don't you think?'

'Wow, none of that had occurred to me.'

'There's also a nice reference for art historians in the use of the mannequins. The surrealists used them, so did the Dadaists. Just not with the genitalia. They shocked the media in the early twentieth century, too.'

'Thanks for the lesson in art appreciation.' Mark genuinely meant it; he wasn't being facetious.

Arthur seemed to realise and carried on. 'A lot of art is to do with taking something out of its normal setting and context. In that way it becomes art rather than just the thing doing what it normally does. Like a mannequin in an art gallery rather than a shop window where you would normally see it. It would normally be wearing clothes, too, so the nakedness again is not something you would normally see.'

'Right.'

'What do you think of it now?'

'Well, I'm not laughing, but I do understand what you mean.' Mark often found jokes a little difficult to understand. He knew he could be a little naïve sometimes as well. Johnny often wound him up about it. 'Never mind the genitals on the faces. More than that, as you say, they're very naked. They look defenceless.' Mark found their vulnerability disturbing.

'I think that's part of the idea. Children are defenceless, aren't they?'

Mark noticed that Arthur was a little different now that they were on their own; softer somehow, less brash. There were obviously many layers here. He found him physically attractive, too, with his strong jaw, dark features and wild aura. He would like to get to know him rather better.

***

As Sophie realised she would have to negotiate her way down the steps at Quaglino's she regretted wearing her highest heels for the evening. It had only been a short walk from the exhibition in Piccadilly, but she was on the limit of what was possible in these shoes. She had seen Posh Spice wearing a pair of open-toed stilettos, and, even though she wasn't a huge fan of the Spice Girls, she liked Victoria Adams's style and had tracked down a similar pair. While she found the group's pop a bit basic, she admired their message and hoped that the generation of young teens who idolised them took Girl Power to heart.

Sophie looked out over the dining area from the top of stairs. The position provided a view over a large bustling room with a stunning vaulted glass ceiling. The chattering classes were at work in the large room below her, where a clinking, clattering buzz rose up as she and the three boys descended to their table. It had been Henri who had booked the restaurant for the four of them to have dinner after the exhibition. She was pretty sure that Johnny and Mark would have settled for going to the pub, so she appreciated Henri's French influence. Her experience with English men was that they socialised in pubs with food as an afterthought, and French men socialised in bistros, brasseries and restaurants with food the main event. Maybe it was changing a little, she thought, particularly in London, as the number of decent restaurants had multiplied in recent times. The tabloids' Britpop London did seem to have had an influence everywhere.

Terence Conran, the man behind the Habitat shops, had reopened Quaglino's earlier in the decade, and it certainly was very stylish. She had read about people pinching the exquisitely designed Q-shaped ashtrays. She now realised that the Q motif was all around them, on the stair rail, in the glass screens as well as in the ashtrays. They followed an elegantly dressed hostess to their table in the large, vaulted room.

'*J'adore les fruits de mer.* We must eat seafood and drink Chablis. Look at that! *Mais, c'est magnifique!*' Henri was in his element.

Sophie looked at the seafood bar that was piled with lobsters, crabs, oysters and heaps of other smaller molluscs and crustaceans, all sitting on piles of ice dotted with lemons and seaweed. It was quite a sight. The bar was supported by a beautiful green-and-gold mosaic depicting creatures from the sea in pale shades of grey and white.

'It looks fabulous, Henri. I'm not sure about the price, though!' Sophie was conscious that her and Johnny's budget didn't really run to high-end London restaurants.

'We can afford it,' said Johnny. Sophie could tell that Johnny was embarrassed by her mentioning money. She knew they couldn't afford it. She let it go.

'No more discussions of price. I am paying for dinner,' said Henri, 'as long as that means I can order the wine. Maybe some champagne to get started.'

There were no dissenting voices.

'That's very generous, Henri,' said Mark.

'Yes, very,' said Sophie smiling at Henri. He twinkled back.

'More than happy to let you order the wine, mate.' Sophie could tell that Johnny had already managed quite a few glasses at the opening. She let that go, too. She wanted to enjoy herself tonight.

There was a buzz in the room, a hubbub, waiters zipping around with trays held high on their shoulders, cigarette girls with trays of cigarettes and cigars, an attempt to revive the look of the Roaring Twenties. Sophie wasn't sure about the cigarette girls, but the rest she loved. There was even a pianist tinkling unobtrusively in the background. They started to chat about the opening. Everyone seemed enthused, each in their own way.

'Well, this is a bit different to our old poker sessions, guys,' said Johnny. 'We seem to have graduated to culture and fine wines.'

The waiter arrived on cue with a bottle of Pol Roger champagne, a favourite of Henri's apparently.

'*Allez les rosbifs*. Please enjoy a glass of Winston Churchill's favourite champagne.' So not just Henri's drink of choice. Sophie smiled inwardly at the way Henri liked to impose himself.

'Translation please. My school French isn't quite up to it.' Mark was confused.

'They call us *les rosbifs*. The roast beefs. We call them the Frogs. It's a little basic, but it seems to have endured,' said Sophie. Henri allowed himself a chuckle. He seemed to be in high spirits.

'Bravo,' he continued. 'I thought we French normally beat you when it came to art, but that exhibition was quite something.'

'It's not a football match.' Sophie did not enjoy this kind of jingoism; the French ancestry on her mother's side meant she preferred to be impartial.

'At least he's finally giving we Brits a compliment,' said Johnny. 'I can tell you that's a fucking rare event.' Sophie watched the three men laughing and smiled. She liked that they were enjoying themselves but still didn't like the patriotic banter.

She changed the subject. 'Did anyone go into Tracey's tent? I was really moved by it. I liked her, too.'

'I didn't really get it,' said Johnny.

'Maybe it's more of a woman thing,' said Mark.

'I don't think it should be, but your responses are proving me wrong.'

'I loved the shark,' said Henri. 'It has given me some very exciting ideas.' Yes, thought Sophie, she could see how Henri would love the shark; he was a bit of a shark. That was part of his attraction.

'*Dead Dad* gave me a few ideas. Did anyone notice that?' It was unlike Johnny to sound so serious. Sophie realised immediately that it had stirred up thoughts of his absent father.

'It was so real looking, all sad and naked and small. Why was it so small?'

'Maybe if it was full size it just becomes a model of his father's actual corpse. If it's smaller it takes on other meanings.'

'Good point, Sophie. It made me think of my dad.'

'I didn't think you had ever met him,' said Mark.

'No, but that doesn't mean I don't think about him. I don't even know what he looks like, but I still think about him.'

'Of course. I'm sorry, Johnny. That was a bit thoughtless.' Mark looked a little embarrassed.

'No worries, man. You were not to know. It made me think I wouldn't want to just find out one day that he had died without ever having met him. Anyway, chin-chin, guys, let's enjoy the champagne.'

'I had a bit of a guided tour from Arthur,' said Mark. Sophie thought he seemed a little self-conscious saying this. 'He certainly opened my eyes to art appreciation. You know that piece by Jake and Dinos with all the shop mannequins kind of welded together?

I was appalled by it at first, the genitals on their faces, the nudity of the kids, but Arthur made me think a bit harder about it.'

'It was good to see Jake and Dinos. I'm not sure about their art, though.' Johnny had not had the art appreciation lesson yet.

'Arthur told me to think of it as a kind of joke. It's so extreme that it can only be funny. Anyone who is shocked and appalled by it has missed the point. They're taking it too literally. Arthur thinks it's intended to expose hypocrisy,' Mark continued.

'Shit, Arthur did well in half an hour. He's turned a philistine into a culture vulture.' Johnny was teasing Mark now.

'It seems there is hope for everyone,' Henri interjected, looking Sophie in the eyes as he did so.

They relented on Mark and began to talk about what they were going to order. Sophie's mind turned to a trip to Paris. She was slightly dumfounded how the tent had provoked her to think of Juste. She had confided in Juste when she had found out about Johnny and Mark, and Juste had given her a very straightforward piece of advice: in life people are sexually attracted to one another; gender is often not relevant. Going to Paris might mean another hook up with Henri, too, but was she more interested in seeing Juste or Henri? And where did that leave her and Johnny, and, for that matter, Amy. Amy was the most important person in her life. She was confused. Best to park the Paris trip for the evening and enjoy the moment.

WATER LILIES

OCTOBER 1997

Johnny lay in bed on an autumnal morning, the sun streaming through the curtain trying to rouse him. Sophie was already up, and he could hear her downstairs chatting with Amy. He would have to get up soon, as Sophie would be going to the shop in Rye and Amy had to be taken to school. These drowsy, short lie-ins were productive creative minutes for him, and he wanted to draw it out a little longer before getting out of bed. He'd had a chord progression running around his head for a couple of weeks, since the exhibition, and now he could feel some words coming:

Naked when you're born
Naked when you die

It was the *Dead Dad* theme rattling around in there. He reached for the Dictaphone that he kept by the side of the bed for such moments and began to speak into it.

I have no memory of entering the world
My mum was there but my dad was missing
I have no memory of entering the world
My mum was there but my dad was missing

He had unconsciously started to sing rather than speak the words. A melody was coming together.

I have no memory of my dad on a slab
I don't wish him dead, that would be sad
I just want to connect, I just want to see him
I just want to see him alive
Naked when you're born
Naked when you die
Naked when you're born
Naked when you die

Sophie put her head around the door. 'Sorry, Johnny, can you take over with Amy? I have to get to the shop.'

'OK, babe.'

He would have to stop for the moment, but he had the makings of something. He just needed to kick it around with his guitar. He could really do with more tunes under his belt to get his solo career further off the ground. The session-type projects he was asked to perform from time to time paid the rent but no more than that. He knew he had a big hit in him, he just had to try to be patient and let it happen. He hummed the *Naked* idea to himself. He could call the song *Naked*. It was one of the things that had stayed with him about *Dead Dad*, the nakedness.

As he showered and dressed, his mind returned to the issue of his own father. As he was growing up, his mother Mary just shut down when he tried to discuss him with her. All he knew was that the relationship had been short and sweet, and then his father had left. He didn't even know if his father left before or after he was born. His mother made the odd, rare comment about her father's shortcomings, but there had been probably fewer than a handful of these over the course of his lifetime. The most recent had come when he had visited her at the height of Swerve's fame when he was a little lost in Jack Daniels and charlie. His visits were infrequent at the time, and it had hurt him when she had made a passing comment comparing his drinking to his father's. He felt uncomfortable about the idea of asking his mother directly for more information. It occurred to him that his gran, his mother's mother, might be a good alternative source of information. She must have been around when his father was on the scene. Both his mother and his gran had lived in Hastings all their lives. His gran lived not far from his mother in a little council house. He had fond but distant memories of his grandad, who had died when he was a small boy; since then, his gran had lived on her own in the same house where his mother had grown up. She had been there since the fifties, part of the war generation. Mary had been an only child, born just after the war. There had not been any brothers and sisters, and Johnny had never asked why, so he had grown up mainly with his mum and his gran, who had showered him in maternal and grandmaternal love. Sophie had commented in the past that he had been spoiled by the women in his life until he had met her, and she was probably right. But he liked it. He couldn't change the past either, the past had made him who he was. He would never say that directly to Sophie as it would piss her off, but that was the reality. He pulled on a Radiohead T-shirt, a pair of slightly baggy and battered Levi 501s and tied up his Converse High Tops. He needed to go and see his gran, soon.

***

Sophie pootled along the Udimore Road towards Rye in her 1975 VW Beetle. Their house in the village of Brede was only a few miles from her shop in Rye; this was her happy place, and she always enjoyed the drive over there. She had been pleased to see Johnny using his Dictaphone this morning, a good sign that he was in an industrious frame of mind. She had noticed that he seemed to have been on an upward trajectory for the last couple of weeks. His boozing was under control, and his general demeanour suggested that he had kicked the coke habit, except for the occasional London binge. He was so much nicer to live with when he was like this. She knew that he missed the short-lived taste of fame he had enjoyed with Swerve, but she didn't miss it at all; it had all been a bit of a car crash for their little family. Anyway, that was in the past. In the future, the near future, was her trip to Paris. It was arranged now for next week. All she had to do was buy her Eurostar ticket down the road at the travel agent in the High Street, and she was ready to go. It was so easy to get to Paris now that they had opened the Eurostar station at Ashford International. She had called Juste and arranged to see her and Véronique at VJ, their wonderful fashion boutique the market at Porte de Clignancourt. She had been buying from them for a few years now, and they had become firm friends. She had confided in Juste when things had been difficult with Johnny, and this had given them an intimacy that sometimes Sophie felt, had the potential to tip over into the sexual. She felt that Juste somehow brought her out of herself, allowing her to discuss her innermost thoughts. Juste had even made a pass at her a while back, and, although she had resisted, mostly out of a sisterly solidarity with Véronique, she knew that she might not be able to do so if it happened again. Her feelings for Juste aside, simply the idea of buying some of their stock for her own shop always excited her, but she was doubly excited this time to be able to tell them all about the tent and Tracey Emin. She had spoken to them to confirm, and she had also spoken to Henri, on his new mobile phone, or *portable*, as he called it. It had been a very short call with Henri as he had warned her of the cost of an international call to a mobile phone. The plan was that they would all meet for dinner that evening following her visit to VJ; it was, of course, Henri who had originally introduced her to Juste and Véronique, and they remained firm friends. She had also decided she was going to get the first train from Ashford to Paris so as to be nice and early, sufficiently early to give herself a little treat before she went to VJ. Amy would be with Johnny for a couple of days, which was fine. Despite everything, he was a very good father. She had realised that having not grown up with one he understood the importance of the role. She smiled to herself as she chugged along towards Rye, the English Channel on her right and the River Tillingham on her left, Paris less than two hundred miles away; she could almost smell the River Seine.

***

'So, if I organised a trip somewhere, would you come?'

'That would depend on where it was, and what you wanted of me.'

Mark found Arthur hard to work out. It was the third time that they had met since the exhibition, and that had only been a couple of weeks earlier. The second occasion had led to Arthur coming back to Mark's flat on Highbury Fields for sex. Mark knew that Arthur found him attractive, not because he had told him but only really because of the sex. Mark admitted to himself that he was not great at reading people anyway, so that made it even harder when someone was a bit of a closed book. Mark had initiated their meetings each time, and Arthur had said yes to each so far. The meetings had taken the same shape; they had met for a few beers in the Compton Arms, close to Mark's flat. Arthur lived down in Shoreditch, so it was not far for him to come. He seemed to be single but seemed to have a reluctance to discuss his personal life in any way. As Mark was not much of a one for discussing his own personal life either, their conversations took a different direction. They talked about culture, a lot about art, but also about music, where Mark knew more and felt he could contribute.

'Well, I was thinking of spending a couple of days in Paris.'

'Now you're talking.'

'Henri contacted me. He lives in Paris, as you might remember.

We've done some business together in the past. He suggested I come over to talk about some stuff.'

In fact, when Mark had spoken to Henri he had mentioned that he had seen Arthur since the exhibition, and Henri had been very interested. He had suggested he bring Arthur to Paris with him.

'He's offered to sort a hotel out for us.'

'Who's paying? I'm pretty skint, mate.'

'I'm not sure about that yet, but don't worry, I can cover the expenses if Henri doesn't.'

'Well then, you're on. I fuckin' love Paris.' Mark smiled. Now he had spent more time with him he had noticed how Arthur worked up his accent for emphasis. Mark did wonder how genuine it was. 'What are your favourite galleries, Mark?'

Mark felt himself frowning. He knew he did this when he wasn't sure what to say or if he was embarrassed. He felt himself doing it when he tried to bluff at poker, but he fought against it.

'I've been to the Louvre. On a school trip in 1981. There was no pyramid at the entrance at that time. I haven't seen that. I haven't been back since then. I've never travelled much; I'm not sure why. My last long-term girlfriend, Victoria, had a family property in Cornwall, so we would go there in the summer. I don't tend to go on holiday alone. The odd trip to watch a test match or see friends. That's about it.'

'You've got a lot to see then, Mark. We're going to have to pack a lot in to a couple of days.'

'Well, the day we arrive I've arranged to meet Henri late afternoon at his bank. If we got the early train we'd have some time do something before the meeting. Then we'll have the evening and the next day if we get a late train back.'

'That's enough to get started. I'll keep it limited to the essentials. There's one place you have to go.'

'Where's that?'

'I'm not saying yet.'

'I'm not that keen on surprises, Arthur.'

'Tough shit, matey. We'll go there first. Straight off the train.'

'OK. I'll just have to trust you.'

'Yes, you will. It's an art gallery, Mark, not a bungee jump from the Eiffel Tower. I just don't want you to start reading about it before we go. I want to see what your immediate reaction to it is. Another pint?'

'Yes please.' Mark downed what remained of his pint of London Pride and handed the empty glass to Arthur, who went up to the bar to order. It was unusual for him to do something unplanned. He felt quite light headed and a little unmoored. He knew it was only a gallery, but normally, if he went somewhere either alone or accompanied, he would have a clear itinerary. Arthur was having an impact on him. He hoped this trip wasn't too much too soon. The only person he might normally have discussed Arthur with was Johnny, but he felt he couldn't do that. Even though what he and Johnny had together was casual, telling him about Arthur would be an uncomfortable conversation. Normally, if he was seeing another man, or woman for that matter, he wouldn't have hidden it from Johnny. He would have felt happy openly discussing it, knowing that it wouldn't impinge on what they had together. This felt different.

***

Johnny loved feeling the wind on his face. An old school friend, Sam Fryer, who had become an RAF pilot, had told him that the only way to recreate the same adrenalin buzz when he wasn't flying a jet was riding a motorbike. Johnny had dabbled in motorbikes in the early eighties, owning a Yamaha FS1E – or Fizzy, as everyone called them – bought not long after his sixteenth birthday, followed by a Yamaha RD250, acquired shortly after his seventeenth birthday. They had both been past-their-best seventies bikes, but he had loved them. There was nothing like the smell of a high-revving two-stroke engine. He had passed both his motorbike and car tests when he was eighteen, partly funded by his gran. His late teens and early twenties had seen him skint and without transport, but once Swerve had taken off he had bought a car pretty quickly, a Peugeot 205 1.9 litre GTi, the hottest of the hot hatches. But the motorbike itch had stayed with him. When he had hooked up with Sam and talked with him about bikes, he had decided to scratch the itch. He had agreed with Sophie that he wouldn't buy a crazily fast sports bike and had decided on a Triumph Bonneville, a 1967 from his birth year, resplendent in an aubergine-and-Alaskan-white petrol tank. It was thirty years old, it wasn't super quick and it wasn't super reliable, but he loved it and had spent the last few months pottering around on it. He had found an open-faced Union Jack crash helmet, to complete his Britpop look, and was now buzzing along the St Leonards seafront enjoying the autumn sunshine, eyes protected by a pair of retro-look Rayban metal-framed shades. Past the pier and then Warrior Square, past the much maligned and vandalised statue of Queen Victoria, past Marine Court, that crazy art deco block of flats designed to resemble a 1930s cruise liner, he continued westwards. He felt like the cock of the walk as he finally changed down the gears with his right foot and steered the bike from the Bexhill Road right into Harley Shute Road and on to another right turn into Edinburgh Road.

He pulled up outside his gran's pebble-dash council house. She had managed to buy it in the eighties, and had changed the front door, but otherwise it remained the same semi-detached house he had been coming to all his life. It sat high above the English Channel, with a view across to France from the front of the house. France was apparently visible only on a very rare, pristine, clear day, which Johnny had never witnessed and believed might be apocryphal. It was, however, a view that punched well above the weight of the housing stock. Johnny had appreciated it more and more as he got older and began to understand the value of location and outlook. On a sunny day like today it made his heart sing. He pulled the Bonneville on to its centre stand, took off his helmet and walked up the path to the door, which his gran opened on cue, smiling at him as he approached.

'I wish you wouldn't ride that bloody motorbike,' she said by way of greeting. 'You know your mum doesn't like you doing it, and I bet Sophie doesn't either.'

'I'm young and irresponsible, Gran. What can I say?'

'Well, I know where you get that from, and it's not from your mother.'

She kissed his cheek as he entered the house. Connie Jones was tough on the outside but soft on the inside, and Johnny knew his way to the soft centre. Johnny and his mother had inherited their blue eyes and good bones from his gran's side of the family. There was a rumour of a Scandinavian link, but nothing had been verified. Johnny's grandad, the original Johnny Jones, had died many years ago now, in the seventies, and he had vague but sweet memories of him. A Welshman by birth, he had worked as an actor and musician and had met Connie just after the Second World War while working in Hastings. The birth of Mary, Johnny's mother, had followed about a year after. The affection that Johnny had enjoyed from Connie and Mary had been a constant in his life. He knew it had made him a little self-centred, but his had been a happy childhood. However, there had been something missing, and it was the absence of his father that he was finally intent on putting right.

'Where would that be from then, Gran?' he asked.

'Never you mind. Come on through. I've made some cake. I'll just put the kettle on.'

These kinds of remarks from his gran as to where he might have acquired a certain element of his personality from had been quite frequent as he grew up, but there was never any more meat on the bone. He was given a glimpse of his father's character traits but nothing more. In the past this had never particularly bothered him, but the sculpture *Dead Dad* had awakened a feeling of emptiness within. What if his own father was already dead? He had realised that he had always thought that at some point he would just reappear, so why hadn't he? Johnny had even become a little bit famous for a while. Still nothing. Maybe he was dead, and his mum and his gran just hadn't told him. Maybe they didn't know.

They walked through to the back kitchen, which always smelled of freshly baked cake with an undercurrent of bleach. His gran wore a blue Nylon housecoat with a floral frock underneath and a pair of floral-patterned slippers. She was quite tall for her generation, and still slim, but slightly bent over from a life of cooking, cleaning and pottering around the house. She lived for her daughter and her grandson and had always been there for them as long for as Johnny could remember. He had seen her several times a week while growing up, at first always with his mother then later alone when he walked the ten minutes or so from their flat in the Bexhill Road on his own. His gran had always operated an open-door policy; there was never any need to let her know he was coming. He had often turned up with a guitar as a teenager, practising his craft as his gran busied herself around the house. In the last few years his visits had become fewer, and he normally called ahead rather than just dropping by, but he felt equally at ease in her company.

'So, to what do I owe the honour?'

'Come on, Gran, it's just a social call. I hadn't seen you for a while, so I thought I'd drop in.'

'I know you better than that.'

'Well, it's a lovely day for a motorbike ride.'

'You'll have to do better than that, too.'

'OK, Gran, I know there's no getting past you.'

Connie harrumphed. She was good at it.

'I went to an exhibition a couple of weeks ago, and I saw a sculpture that I can't get out of my mind.'

'Really?' His gran sounded disappointed that he might have called round to discuss a sculpture.

'Yes, really. It was called *Dead Dad*.' He sensed he'd piqued her interest. 'It was a model of the artist's naked dead father.'

'Well, that doesn't sound right. Why would anyone want to look at that?'

'Apparently it was made from memory rather than from photographs. It's not full size, it's about two-thirds size. It's colour. It looks quite real. I found it haunting.'

His gran harrumphed again. She was not taking the bait yet. He would have to spell it out. She slurped her tea.

'It made me think of my own father.' He had said it. The cat was out of the bag. There was a silence.

'I knew this would come eventually. In fact, I'm surprised it's taken this long. I suppose it's only natural.'

'Well, it's just not something I can discuss with Mum. She just clams up. Apart from the oblique references you both make to the character defects I inherited from him, I know nothing about him. I don't even know his name.'

'His name's Marty Brown. Funnily enough he's an artist of sorts. He lives in Brighton.'

'What?' Johnny could not believe what he had just heard. He was staggered that the information was so easy to come by, and more staggered that his father lived so close by.

'It's time you knew. I haven't got the heart to keep it from you any more. I'll have to tell your mother I've told you, too. That won't be easy. She hadn't exactly sworn me to secrecy, but she won't be happy.'

'He's been down the road in Brighton all this time?'

'As far as I know. I haven't seen him for thirty years either. He didn't hang around for long once he knew your mum was pregnant. He was only a young lad himself, I suppose. I knew his parents vaguely; they lived in Bexhill. They both passed away a few years ago.'

'What? The grandparents I never knew?' Johnny could scarcely believe what he was hearing.

'I'm not sure that they knew either. Marty skipped town as soon as he found out, went on the so-called hippy trail apparently, then turned up in Brighton a few years later. I honestly don't know much more than that myself. Your mother might know a bit more, but we never speak about it. I only met Marty a few times back in the sixties. He was a charmer, all right, but callow. He may have been scared of your grandad, and he'd have been right to be. It was tough in those days to bring a child up out of wedlock.'

There was a knock at the door followed by a familiar voice. 'Hello, love, I thought that looked like your bike.' Mary, Johnny's mother, had let herself in right on cue. 'What's up? You look a bit pale. There's nothing wrong is there?'

The subject of Marty Brown would remain closed for the moment. Johnny couldn't face confronting his mother quite yet. He got up to give her a hug.

'Nothing's wrong, Mum. I was just telling Gran about the contemporary art exhibition I went to in London a couple of weeks ago.'

'You've always been interested in art. It's not so surprising really,' Mary said.

Another oblique reference that he now understood.

'Wasn't that the exhibition with the picture of that hateful woman Myra Hindley?'

'Yes, Mum. She may be a hateful person, but that doesn't make the art hateful, does it?'

'Well, that might be your opinion, but all I can think of when that name comes up is the mothers and fathers of those poor murdered kids.'

***

Henri had spent a lot of time sitting on this terrace over the years, first as a teenager, then as an undergraduate, drinking small glasses of *pression* beer, laughing with his friends. He could see their faces now. The terrace at La Clémence in the Old Town of Geneva, Place du Bourg-de-Four, always brought it all back. The ghosts from the past gradually melted away as he sipped on his coffee and returned his thoughts to the present.

He lit up a Disque Bleu and inhaled the acrid smoke from the dark tobacco deeply into his lungs. He was a little early for his appointment at the gallery around the corner. Since he left Geneva under a cloud nearly three years ago, he had made regular trips back to keep in touch with his network, see friends and to rekindle his on–off relationship with Emily. She was based back in Geneva now, which suited him better than London in many ways. He had spent the previous night with her, and could still smell her, that smell that always reminded him of summer in Aix-en-Provence, oranges and rosemary. He was strongly attracted to her physically, but mentally he found her too compliant, too eager to please, too nice. He knew he would never commit to her, but she seemed to accept that. He knew she had other boyfriends from time to time, but it was rare that she would tell him that she couldn't see him when he appeared out of nowhere at short notice. He would keep calling her as long as it suited him. He would keep seeing Sophie, too, again not because he wanted any permanence in their relationship, but because she excited him. Johnny had not held any grudge against him for his past affair with Sophie; that wasn't his way. Even so, Henri was discreet about it, and he assumed that Sophie was, too. He was sure that Johnny knew that he and Sophie met in Paris from time to time, and their next meeting was coming up in a few days. The only snag was that it coincided with the visit of Mark and Arthur that he had organised. Sophie had called about her own trip to see Juste and Véronique shortly afterwards. He hadn't told Sophie about Mark and Arthur coming yet; he knew that, other than the get-together on New Year's Eve 1994, Mark and Sophie hadn't really seen much of one another since the infamous poker game in Lausanne, where he had been outed by Mark as Sophie's lover, and he hadn't wanted to put her off. Although they seemed to have buried any animosity for the trip to the *Sensation* exhibition, he knew that it was probably on a gentle simmer under the surface. He would deal with any difficulty in a few days when they all arrived.

What he needed to think about for the next hour or so was his meeting at La Galerie Schmidt. He had grown up with Caroline Schmidt, who, like him, had Parisian parents, only hers were art dealers. They had a gallery in Paris and a gallery in Geneva and commuted between the two, latterly spending more time in Geneva than Paris, as they had thought that Caroline would receive a more international education there. This they had hoped would prepare her to succeed them in running the two galleries. This plan had at least partially come to fruition as Henri was about to meet Caroline in her capacity as the relatively new head of the Geneva business. This newfound responsibility was a long way from their carefree youthful excursions to the terrace of La Clémence where he currently sat, but geographically the gallery lay just down the road in the heart of Geneva's Old Town. It was not just any old gallery. The window display was quite likely to include a Picasso or a Monet, something that Henri had accepted growing up but now realised was not the norm for a high-street gallery. Geneva had always punched above its weight; it was a small city with a very wealthy population, and Henri loved it for that.

Since *Sensation* he had not been able to shake the image of the shark from his mind. His attempts to connect with Damien Hirst following the exhibition had so far fallen on stony ground, but Hirst was only one of the new breed of artists as Henri saw it. He was convinced that this movement, Britart as some people were calling it, or the YBAs he had also heard, was about to explode on to the global art scene. He wanted a piece of it. When he had called Mark to discuss how they might go about making some money from it, he had been surprised but pleased to learn that Mark seemed to have cultivated Arthur Swale. This had led to their invitation to Paris and now the meeting with Caroline.

He drained his coffee, extinguished the Disque Bleu and left three Swiss francs on the table before setting off across the square and down the Grande Rue. The Old Town stood high above the city, its ancient, tall, stone buildings castings shadows over the narrow streets. Despite its familiarity, this part of Geneva always evoked a sense of history in Henri; his childhood had been spent here celebrating the Fête de l'Escalade, the annual holiday in December that celebrated the victory over the invading Savoyard troops in the 1600s. The Mère Royaume was alleged to have repelled them by throwing a cauldron of soup over them from her vantage point at the top of the city ramparts. This was now remembered by the locals in the form of edible chocolate soup cauldrons and marzipan vegetables every 11 December. While the land around the city walls had changed enormously since 1602, the Old Town itself had largely remained the same, with its narrow, cobbled streets, large dark stone buildings and a certain sense of foreboding. The walls still stood proud above the rest of the city looking out towards the Jura mountains to the west, the River Rhône to the south and the Alps to the east. It was easy to see why the Savoyards wanted to invade; the city was a perfect vantage point at the foot of Lac Léman. Instead, the invasion had been more subtle, and it had been financial. Since the 1700s Geneva had established itself as a financial centre, and it was money that had taken over during the subsequent three centuries. The finest art had always attracted money, and in the same way money had always attracted the finest art. In Geneva the money had come first, followed by the art. One could argue, Henri thought, that with Britart, the money had not arrived yet, but it would, one way or another, and that was what he wanted to put to Caroline.

He buzzed at the gallery entrance and pushed the door as he heard it unlock. Just a small buzzer, nothing as elaborate as a camera or intercom. This world preferred security to be discreet. In the window next to the door was what to Henri looked like a Picasso, surrealist period, probably 1930s, he thought, concentrating on the naked female form, which, in its curved, abstract way, was striking in its simplicity, but with a humorous touch, too. Henri was not an expert, but he knew what he liked, and he liked Picasso. One day he hoped to come to Caroline as a customer as well as an old friend. As he entered the shop she appeared, tall and blonde, with well-sculpted features, blue eyes and bright-red lips, the latter courtesy, Henri assumed, of Chanel.

'Henri, it's so nice to see you.'

'The pleasure is all mine, Caroline.'

They spoke in French, as they had done at school, although they could equally have communicated in English. She wore an elegant black suit – also Chanel if he was not mistaken – nipped in at the waist, with dark sheer tights and black patent pumps. These looked Italian to Henri. Ferragamo maybe? He took all this in as he kissed her on both cheeks. For many in Geneva it was three kisses as a greeting, but Henri knew it would be two kisses with Caroline, *à la parisienne*. Three would have been considered somewhat vulgar. He vaguely remembered kissing her on the mouth once or twice back in the old days, but nothing further had developed. She had always been a little out of his league.

He followed her through to a small office at the back of the gallery. Space was still at a premium at an exclusive address like this, even if the items being sold ran into multiple millions. He took the seat she offered opposite her at her desk.

A good-looking man in his early twenties wearing a dark, well-cut suit popped his head around the door as they sat down in the office.

'Can I offer you something to drink?' he asked.

'I'll have an espresso please,' said Henri.

'Just water for me, Jean-Pierre, thank you.'

Henri never refused a coffee. The caffeine kept him alert. He could see that Caroline was running the operation like a well-oiled machine. This was what the super-rich expected. Even when they had plenty of time on their hands, in Henri's experience, the very wealthy liked to give the impression that they were frantically busy, moving from one important appointment to another throughout the day. This meant that those serving them, like their private bankers and art dealers, also had to give that impression. The well-oiled machine was a function of this process, offering a vision of efficiency. Many of those who served the very wealthy had their own ambitions to become as wealthy as their clientele. Caroline's family had reached that point already; Henri was still on the ladder, but he spent his time observing and absorbing their habits.

'I'm sorry, but I only have around half an hour, Henri. I have a customer coming to view a painting.'

Right on cue, thought Henri. While he was sure that Caroline *was* busy and *did* have a meeting, setting the amount of time that she had allocated to him at half an hour was a little demeaning.

'I'll keep it short and to the point.'

Henri produced the Royal Academy's glossy coffee-table book on the *Sensation* exhibition from his bag and put it on Caroline's desk.

'I was at the *vernissage* for this exhibition last month. It blew me away. This is the future of art, Caroline, and I will be able to give you exclusive access to one of the artists.'

'Ah, yes, Charles Saatchi's students,' said Caroline.

'They may have been students when he started buying their art, but they're not students now. This movement is really taking off.'

'I can see that some of this work might be commercial for the right customer, but I'm not sure that we have those customers. Our clientele is pretty conservative; most of our sales are of art produced between about 1850 and 1970, impressionists, cubists, abstract expressionists, surrealists, maybe even some pop art, but nothing this contemporary.'

'Don't you have to look to new markets to keep growing your business? I really believe this Britart movement will raise the profile of contemporary art in general. It will create new buyers in the market. People who can't afford a Picasso or a Dalí or even a Warhol, what can they buy? Lesser-known dead artists or something new and vibrant that has the potential to grow exponentially in value? Damien Hirst is already a hot property, for example.'

'The dead cows.'

'Yes, although I prefer the sharks.' Caroline smiled at him ruefully. She was thumbing through the *Sensation* book.

'So, what could you offer me if I was interested? Something by Hirst? The Chapman Brothers? Rachel Whiteread?'

'The artist I have an exclusive arrangement with is Arthur Swale.'

'I don't know him.'

'There's a photo of his sculpture *The Narcissist* in the book. It's the one where the page is turned down at the corner.'

Caroline turned to the page and looked quizzically at the photograph of the metal sculpture. 'Really? You think the customers of La Galerie Schmidt want to have a sculpture of a man pissing in his own mouth in their salon?'

'I know it's provocative, but there is a toughness in the construction that is very attractive. I think it's witty, too. Brutal but whimsical at the same time.'

'The vocabulary of art criticism seems to come easily to you, Henri!' Caroline was smiling at him again, mocking him a little, but there was warmth in the smile. 'I'm not sure about the art. I'll have to make some enquiries, but I do agree with what you say about attracting a newer younger clientele. I've been pondering this myself for a little while. I'm not sure Geneva is ready for it, but maybe Paris. I would have to work on my parents, but there might be something in it.'

'Let me know what your maman and papa say. I'm convinced there is something in this, Caroline.'

'You may be right. There's not too much downside, other than reputational. I'll think about the terms. My markup would need to be higher than usual for a new artist, given that we would be taking a big reputational risk.'

'That would not be a problem.' Henri would need to negotiate hard with Swale at their meeting in Paris. He would also need to sell a solo exhibition at Galerie Schmidt in Paris as a fait accompli. He hoped Swale had some other work; so far he had only seen *The Narcissist*. He was taking some reputational risk himself, but he was convinced he could pull both ends of this deal off.

***

Sophie climbed the stairs out of the Concorde *métro* and was greeted by the soft, late-autumn sun gently kissing her face. She looked across the grand expanse of the Tuileries Garden, and suddenly she felt strangely at home, the familiarity of the view evoking a strong feeling of connection in her. She was excited about the whole trip, but catching the early train meant that she could visit her most favourite place in the whole city, the Musée de l'Orangerie containing Monet's *Water Lily* paintings. She carried only a small backpack with a change of underwear and shoes; her blue floral-print minidress and white denim jacket would have to serve as day and night wear. She would put on her heels when they met up with Henri later. She had remembered how much she ended up walking in Paris, so was sporting her black Converse during the day. Even what looked like a short distance on the map always seemed to turn out to be longer; the Garden was huge and so different when compared with, say, a London park. Most of the paths were gravel, and the dust and dryness they created was something that reminded her that she was in Paris, that and the fact that the temperature was always a degree or two warmer.

She thought about the paintings as she walked over to the Musée. She had taken an art-history course in the sixth form that had been taught by one of her favourite teachers, Miss Bourne, a genuine sixties hippy with a real passion for art; she had turned her on to the impressionists, and Monet in particular. It had been a surprise to her when she had learned that he had died in 1926, eight years after the First World War had ended. Somehow her vague idea of impressionism to that point had placed it in the previous century. She had not been altogether wrong, as the bulk of Monet's famous paintings were painted during the nineteenth century, and these were the ones that she had been aware of as she grew up, colourful images of poppy fields, wheat stacks and Victorian-looking ladies with parasols. But she had been taught that he had carried on painting right to the end of his life, despite his failing eyesight, with his work becoming more and more abstract as he aged. The huge canvases at the Musée had been donated by him to commemorate the lives of those men lost in the Great War that had only just ended. They were all based on the famous lily ponds at his home in Giverny, Normandy. She had first seen projected slides of the canvases in one of Miss Bourne's lessons and had been captivated by their colours and shapes; it had prompted her to travel to Paris with friends that same teenage summer to view the paintings. She smiled as she thought of herself and her friends, Sally and Jane, travelling to Paris by ferry and train, with their big eighties hair and baggy Levi's pinched in at the waist by thick belts; they had been like a post-adolescent Bananarama. It had been more than ten years since that time. She had changed her hairstyle to a short glossy bob not long after that trip. It had made her feel more sophisticated, but sometimes she missed the naïve enthusiasm of her late-teenage self.

She walked around the sweeping curves of the paths that led

up to the gallery entrance and felt quite moved by the anticipation of what lay within. Moments like this were few and far between since she had become responsible for Amy and married Johnny. Just having the time to indulge herself in some introspection meant everything sometimes; she could escape her normal world of responsibility and mundanity for a couple of days then return to it refreshed and invigorated. She approached the building and took in its simple classical lines and brutal size; it was hard to think that it had been built originally as an orangery and had housed fruit for decades before becoming a gallery. She knew that at the time it was built, the side of the building facing the Seine to her right had been made of glass to magnify the sunlight and ripen the oranges. When it was converted to a museum, the glass wall was replaced with solid stone, transforming the building, Sophie thought, into one that resembled a classical temple, a temple to the arts.

She bought her ticket, ignored the signs to the rest of the collection and hurried through to the two oval rooms that contained the huge Monet canvases. These were fixed four to a room to curved walls, adding a continuity as each painting somehow flowed into the next. Her timing was good, as it was approaching lunchtime, and the French were eating or preparing to eat rather than visiting museums, leaving Sophie almost alone in the first of the rooms where there was just a sprinkling of other tourists. She went straight to the seats in the middle and faced one of her favourites of the eight paintings, the *Soleil Couchant*, the *Setting Sun*. It had probably the most varied colour palate of any of the paintings, ranging from a fierce yellow, through pinks, mauves, purples and greens. It reminded her of Johnny somehow, a turbulent, fiery image of the reflected sun in the centre that gradually reduced intensity to more peaceful, muted-coloured images of the lily ponds on the outside. She liked Johnny's fiery side, provided the fire was natural rather than induced by a heavy night. It was that fire, she thought, that often gave people creativity.

After some time she stood up and moved around the room by one hundred and eighty degrees to the opposite end, to sit in front of the painting called *Reflets Verts*, *Green Reflections*. She liked the puzzle in this image of working out which was the reflection and which was the reality, and in doing so her eyes became lost in the colour and abstraction of the image, almost falling into it. It made her think of Henri. Was he in love with her? She doubted that. Did he even like her? Probably, but she never really knew what he was thinking, even in their most intimate moments. Was it just a game to him, like when he played poker? A way to show off to his friends, almost to belittle them? Was he only really doing it to humiliate Johnny? She would be seeing him later; would they sleep together again? Did she want to? Right now she felt as if the answer was no. She would see how she felt later. Juste and Véronique had offered to put her up at their apartment tonight, and she had taken them up on that; it would make it rather obvious to them if she went home with Henri instead.

She stood up and moved to stand for a while in front of *Matin*, *Morning*, and *Les Nuages*, *The Clouds*, the other paintings in the first of the two specially designed oval rooms. These were lighter, stiller images, and she felt as if a weight had been lifted when she looked at each of them in turn. It made her think of Amy, of Juste and Véronique, whom she'd be with later, and, to her surprise, even her mother. She felt the lightness of other women, the solidarity of the relationships, the lack of that underlying sexual demand that came with relationships with men. All her relationships with women had their complications, but to date they had not had a sexual element. Somehow this made things easier. She was surprised when she found herself thinking again of Tracey Emin's tent, the strength that it took to present yourself to the world so publicly, knowing that she would be damned for doing so. It reminded her of the subtlety of the play on the words *Slept With* in the title of the work, the memories it evoked of sleeping with your mother as a child or your friends at a sleepover, as well as more sexual exploits.

She contemplated this for a while longer while sitting in front of *Les Nuages*. Then she stood up and moved into the second room, which housed the four remaining paintings. She felt as if she was floating a little; it was a wonderful feeling and one that she was amazed could be brought on simply by looking at paintings. She was totally immersed as she entered the room. Her favourite painting here was *Les Deux Saules, The Two Willows*. It was the largest of the eight, and she loved its pink-and-mauve clouds above pale abstract forms of lilies, all framed by the willow trees at each end. She looked towards it at the opposite end of the room, but her view was obscured by two men standing in front of it.

She walked to the right and down the room to try to see around the two guys; she realised, with irritation, that they were speaking English. She had managed to block out the French speakers as she was going around, as she had to concentrate a little to understand what they were saying. The English she understood instinctively.

'This to me is the masterpiece. They are all wonderful paintings, but this one is just so well conceived and so well painted. Look closely at the layering of the paint. It's a master at work.'

The man speaking had a soft northern-English accent. He sounded oddly familiar. She was a few yards away when she stopped in her tracks as she realised. It was the mane of black hair, the parka and the boots. Shit, it was Arthur Swale. What a coincidence! She remained still to avoid being noticed for a moment. Who was that with him? How odd, it was Mark, Mark Arnold, in an art gallery! What was he doing with Arthur? What was he wearing? It looked like a Harrington jacket; a very indie look for Mark. It was teamed with a pair of grey slacks and some work shoes, so the look was not quite complete. That was more like Mark. He turned his head and spotted her immediately.

'Sophie. What are you doing here!' Mark's face coloured as he recognised her. Sophie wondered why? Was it just the surprise of seeing her? Or did he not want to be seen? Mark was frowning a little; that was his poker 'tell'.

'Hi, Mark. I could ask you the same! I never had you down as an art lover.'

'People change,' Arthur interjected. 'Mark's on a journey. We're starting with the very best.' His accent seemed a little more northern than when he'd thought he'd been alone with Mark. The delivery a little harsher. Once again she wondered it was all a bit of an act.

'Hello, Arthur. I'm Sophie. We met at the *Sensation* exhibition.'

'Yes, I remember. Are you all right, duck?'

They all stood a little awkwardly for a moment.

'I'm here on a business trip. I'm buying some clothes for the shop this afternoon from my friends Juste and Véronique up in Clignancourt. I got an early train over to squeeze in a visit here at the Musée. These Monet water lilies are my favourite paintings in Paris – well, anywhere really.'

'Well, you have very good taste then,' said Arthur. Sophie noticed that Mark was smiling at Arthur as he turned to talk to her. There was a lot of admiration in his smile.

'We're on a business trip too,' Mark said. 'We're meeting Henri after this. He wants to talk to Arthur about his art. Apparently, he has a prestigious Parisian gallery interested in hosting an exhibition for Arthur. Someone he knows from his Geneva days.'

'Oh, wow, that sounds pretty amazing. Well done, Arthur. I'm supposed to be seeing Henri later. He introduced me to Juste and Véronique originally. He didn't mention you'd be here, Mark.'

'Well, we're supposed to be going to somewhere called the Buddha-Bar later with him. Maybe we could meet up.' Sophie thought the tone of Mark's invitation was a little reluctant, but she let it pass.

'That's where Henri said that we're going, too. What a happy coincidence! I don't have much time left, so I'm just going to finish looking at the paintings, then I must run. See you at the Buddha-Bar later.'

She extricated herself and walked to the other end of the room. That had been odd. Mark and Arthur Swale. Their body language gave the impression that they were quite familiar with one another, but she was sure that Mark had only been introduced to Arthur at *Sensation* just a few weeks earlier. Johnny hadn't mentioned anything either. Maybe he didn't know that they'd become friends. He seemed to see less of Mark these days. Or maybe Mark was keeping it a bit secret. Were Mark and Arthur an item? Interesting. She wondered guiltily for a moment if Mark might think it was odd that she was seeing Henri later. A few years had passed now since that fateful evening when Mark had blurted out in front of everyone, including Johnny, that she and Henri were sleeping together. She had realised eventually that Mark had never forgiven her for rejecting him at university and later going off with his best friend. Telling Johnny that she and Henri were having an affair had seemed like an act of revenge on Mark's part. Johnny had never held it against her; he hadn't seemed that bothered. They had split up for a while, of course, but that was more to do with the Johnny and Mark thing, as well as Johnny's drink-and-drugs issues. She had thought that she and Mark were just friends as students at UCL, she had thought even then that Mark might be gay, but it had turned out that he had had a crush on her, and she was unable to reciprocate. He had proved that he was bisexual later, with Johnny, but she tried not to think about that any longer. That memory had been wrapped up and put in a locked box, never to be revisited. She felt pretty sure that there was nothing physical between Johnny and Mark now. However, she recognised the guilty look on Mark's face; the more she thought about it the more she thought there was something going on between him and Arthur. She was sure. She was sitting at the other end of the room now, trying to lose herself in *Reflets d'Arbres, Tree Reflections,* the combinations of dark purples in the background, some almost black, contrasting with bright-blue, almost turquoise, lilies that mirrored the turbulence of her thoughts. She wondered why Mark would be hesitant about his relationship with Arthur. She didn't care who he slept with unless it was her husband! As she was having that reflection of her own, they walked past, and Mark waved, mouthing 'see you later' to her. In time all would be revealed. For now, she had to get up to Clignancourt and buy some stock.

***

That was weird, thought Mark. Arthur had a favourite brasserie opposite the Bourse *métro* exit, and they were heading up there on a Line 3 train for a quick lunch before meeting Henri. It was so odd that Sophie had been at the Musée. Mark knew he could be a bit paranoid, but was it credible that Henri had not told her that he and Arthur were going there? Had she followed them? Had she spotted them in London and set the coincidence up? They must have been on the same train. Why would Henri not even tell Sophie that he and Arthur were going to be at the dinner later? Although he had to admit Henri had not told them that Sophie and her two friends would be there either. Maybe it was just Henri being Henri, and there was no more to it than that, and it really had all been a coincidence. He had thought about telling Arthur some of the back story to his relationships with Sophie, Johnny and Henri, but Arthur was not one for personal chat, and Mark did not want to scare him off so soon with that kind of talk. He would ask Henri later. They arrived at Bourse and walked up the steps that led out of the *métro* to Brasserie Vaudeville.

'I'm fuckin' starving,' Arthur said as they walked into the restaurant. He could be a man of few words.

They were shown to their table in the bustling restaurant by an immaculately dressed maître d'hôtel. The servers seemed to be all around them, wearing the traditional French uniform of black bow tie, white shirt and black trousers covered by a long white apron. They moved at speed around the room with large metal trays piled with food and drinks held high above their heads on the flat of one hand. Mark and Arthur were quickly seated at a small banquette in the corner of the room. Mark already had the impression that this place ran like a Swiss watch.

'Right, mate. No need to look at the menus. We're having steak tartare and chips followed by chocolate mousse. And half a kilo of *vin rouge*. Can you translate please.' Mark wasn't sure what steak tartare was, but he decided just to go with the flow. He had been brought up in Hastings on a diet of meat and two veg, since when he had tried to become more adventurous, particularly around people like Arthur and Henri, who seemed to love eating animals from nose to tail. He used his schoolboy French to order what Arthur had asked for. The term half a kilo of wine turned out to be a colloquialism that Arthur had picked up somewhere – it actually meant half a litre – and Mark seemed to score points with the waiter for knowing it.

'So, what's the deal with Sophie?' Arthur had a way of getting straight to the point.

'She's Johnny's wife.'

'Well, I know that already. What's the deal with you and her?'

'There's no deal. We were friends at UCL. She met Johnny through me. We were playing poker when they met, in our old student flat in Wapping. Henri was there, too. I've never asked if you play?'

'There's more to it than that. I could smell an atmosphere between you, but I'll let it pass. Let's talk about the paintings. What did you think?'

Arthur was obviously not interested in poker. It was too soon to give him a potted history of his relationship with Sophie. Mark was pleased that he hadn't pushed him into it but unsure of himself now the subject of conversation had been switched. Cricket, music, the economy, business, he was happy discussing any of these. Art was more difficult. He normally just let Arthur talk about art.

'Well, they were big. Much bigger than I expected.'

'Good point. They are massive, particularly for the era. The canvases would have cost a fortune, and all that oil paint, all those little tubes. Fortunately, Monet was loaded with cash, so not a problem. He had been selling acres of art to the Yanks and the Japanese by the time he got round to doing these, so he was absolutely minted. Apparently he built a special studio, full of pulleys and ladders, just so that he could paint these massive canvases. People forget the practicalities of creating art; it's a big part of it.'

'I can see that. Your sculptures must take a lot of practical planning.'

Arthur was in his element here. Mark listened for a while as he explained the ins and outs of creating a sculpture like *The Narcissist.* He enjoyed listening to Arthur speaking knowledgeably about a subject. It was only the arrival of their food that slowed Arthur down. Mark looked down at his steak tartare. There was a disc of chopped red meat, formed neatly into a perfect circle, topped by what looked like a raw egg yolk. None of it seemed to be cooked. On the side were four small triangles of toast and some chips.

'It's not cooked,' he said to Arthur.

'That's because it's a tartare, mate.'

'I've never eaten raw meat.'

'It's top-quality beef, super-tender, hand cut, seasoned with some capers and mustard and other stuff, topped off with a raw egg yolk. You're supposed to mix the egg yolk into it. You will love it.'

Mark wasn't so sure. He mixed the egg yolk, took a big mouthful of red wine, followed by a forkful of the tartare. It was surprisingly good, soft but a little chewy in texture, with the earthy flavour of the meat elevated by the seasoning and the richness of the egg yolk. Arthur really was teaching him some good things.

'It's delicious.'

'I know. I told you it was.' Arthur grinned at him, and he smiled back. 'Back to Monet,' Arthur said. 'Any other thoughts?'

'Well, they were more abstract than I expected. I knew impressionist paintings were a bit out of focus, but those were very abstract.'

'Again, good observation,' said Arthur. 'There's a practical reason for that, too. Monet's eyesight was fucked for the last twenty years or so of his life. He was in his eighties when he died in the 1920s, and he could hardly see, hence the abstract nature of the paintings. But the brushwork is still magnificent, as is the use of colour and the layering of the paint. He was a master of his craft. He painted every day, trashed stuff he wasn't happy with, ranted and raved. I have a lot to thank him for. I think we're quite similar.'

Mark was never quite sure if Arthur was joking. 'I thought they were great. Thanks for educating me.'

'I can assure you that the pleasure was all mine. So, what about this meeting later? Any thoughts? Business is your area of expertise.'

'Well, as I've said to you before, Henri can be quite tricky, but he's very well connected; it comes as no surprise that he knows the people who own Galerie Schmidt. What he has been asking me is how much other work you have apart from *The Narcissist*. I think he's told the gallery that you have a body of other work to show.'

'Well, yes, I do have other work, but I also may be taking things in a new direction.'

'How so?'

'I'll save that for the meeting. What time is it happening, remind me?'

Mark had noticed that Arthur was not big on keeping track of time. He used Mark to do that, which was fine, as Mark always kept track of time.

'We're due there in forty-five minutes. What do you want to get out of the meeting?'

'Well, I'd like to get an exhibition out of it. You can deal with the money side. That's not my bag. Charles Saatchi has bought most of my work so far, which probably means I've sold it too cheap. But at least I've sold it. You realise he owned all the art at *Sensation*?'

'I hadn't quite worked that out, no. Do we need his permission to show *The Narcissist* in Paris then?'

'Theoretically yes, but that won't be a problem. He's normally happy for the stuff he owns to be shown, as he figures that it increases its value.'

'OK, I understand that. We haven't discussed the money side at all, though. How do I know what you want?'

'I trust you, Mark. I'm sure you'll do your best for me, but I want you to stick to the financials. The art is mine. I don't need your input on that. Is that clear?'

Mark was quite taken aback. He seemed to have been appointed as Arthur's agent.

'Well, when I'm negotiating something like this it helps to have a target to aim for. If you don't have one, I'll try to get them to name their number first then negotiate it in our favour.'

'Sounds like a good plan. As I said, I trust you, Mark, and that sort of thing is not my forte. I just want to concentrate on the art.'

Shortly after they had finished the tartare Mark was presented with the chocolate mousse accompanied by a spoonful of crème fraîche. The brown mousse was slightly reminiscent of a turd, Mark thought. The only chocolate mousse he had tried before had been in a plastic pot.

'I know it looks like a poo, but that shape is called a quenelle. I can assure you it's fuckin' delicious.'

Mark tried it. Arthur was right, it was extraordinary, light and fluffy with a rich taste of dark chocolate. The slightly tart cream was perfect with it. He finished it in a few spoonfuls. Arthur was educating him in ways he had never imagined he would enjoy. It had started with the way that he had opened his eyes to the Chapman Brothers' mannequins and continued every time he was with him. Arthur, he realised, gave him confidence. He was ready to do battle with Henri. He had learned from the poker table that Henri was an adept negotiator, but he was determined to impress Arthur with his own skills.

***

Sophie watched Juste and Véronique as they argued over what to order to drink. Their relationship seemed to be built on these small disagreements. They had decided to stop in a small street-side café near the Buddha-Bar, in the Madeleine district. Henri claimed to have met them many years ago in a lesbian bar in Geneva. She herself had now known them for several years, and they had become firm friends. Juste was the more masculine looking of the two, with her look heavily influenced by Jean-Paul Gaultier. It was a look that she had stayed with all the time that Sophie had known her. She wore her hair short and coloured it peroxide blonde, which somehow emphasised her slim, wiry body encased in a black T-shirt and black jeans, both by Chanel. She exuded a powerful energy that Sophie had always felt drawn to. This was enhanced by the black-leather, thick-soled, lace-up boots she often wore, which encapsulated her no-nonsense attitude. Véronique was the yin to Juste's yang; she had always reminded Sophie of Vanessa Paradis. She was pretty in a bohemian way, with long, soft brown hair, bright-blue eyes and lips that were always the colour of a ripe strawberry. She had an easy style in clothes. Tonight she wore a brown suede miniskirt, almost certainly early-seventies vintage, with a tight-fitting, cropped, green-silk sleeveless top that oozed French couture. Sophie could not immediately guess the labels, but maybe the skirt was English and the top French. These items were complemented by some shabby-chic, hippyish necklaces and pendants and finished by a beautiful pair of up-to-date, knee-length, brown-leather boots with at least a three-inch heel. The boots meant that she rather towered over Juste, but there was no doubt that the shorter of the two was the dominant personality in the relationship. Juste was an incorrigible flirt, and after she had made the pass at Sophie, Véronique had been furious. However, the flirtation almost seemed to have cemented Sophie's relationship with them both. They always spoke French together, which put Sophie at a slight disadvantage, but Véronique's English was slight. Juste, however, was fluent in English as well as French, Russian and Italian – at least these were the languages that Sophie had witnessed her speaking. She was genuine Eurotrash, the daughter of a Russian aristocrat, who had apparently drunk himself to death. Sophie knew little of Juste's mother, only that she did not approve of her sexual preferences and had cut her off.

'I don't like you when you drink pastis. It makes you aggressive.' Véronique was standing her ground.

'Well, I am aggressive. Suck it up.' Juste was giving no quarter, but Sophie suspected she would give way in the end.

'Well, I would like champagne, and it's much nicer if we have a bottle, but that means everyone has to have champagne. Do you mind drinking champagne, Sophie?'

'I love champagne,' she said with a laugh. 'I would definitely rather have it than pastis.'

'*Putain*. You're ganging up on me now. OK. Champagne it is.' Having acquiesced, Juste took charge of the ordering. Sophie loved the way that in Paris it was perfectly normal to order a bottle of champagne in an ordinary street café. Maybe not in the *banlieues*, but in an area like Madeleine no one batted an eyelid.

Once the ordering was done and the champagne delivered, a new line of questioning started.

‘So, we’ve talked about fashion enough for one day.’ Sophie braced herself for what was coming. Juste always cut right to the heart of the matter. ‘This guy Mark, the one you bumped into today, is he the one that was sucking your husband’s cock?’

‘Oh God. I’d tried to forget that I’d told you about that.’ Sophie had buried the fact that the girls knew all about Johnny and Mark and the liaison that had led to Sophie’s temporary separation from Johnny. They had been back together now for about three years she realised. Véronique could not help laughing. She seemed to love it when Juste said the thing that would normally remain unsaid.

‘Well, you told us some stuff, and Henri told us some stuff, and we put two and two together and made five.’ Juste smiled as she talked.

‘Yes, it’s the same Mark that we’re meeting at the Buddha-Bar. We made our peace recently at an art exhibition. You know, I knew Mark before Johnny. I met Mark at university, and we became friends. Actually, he had a bit of a crush on me, but I didn’t feel the same. He introduced me to Johnny at a poker game in London when we were still students, and we hit it off straight away. Mark and Johnny were at school together. Mark never really forgave me for going off with his best friend.’

‘Can we take it that your husband is no longer putting his cock in this Mark’s mouth?’ Véronique was tittering again. It was hard for Sophie to remain serious, even though the thought of what was being discussed normally made her feel a little sick, even several years after she had witnessed it happening.

‘As far as I know it has not happened for a long time. I think Mark has found someone new in any case. I had the impression that he and the artist Arthur were more than friends when I bumped into them earlier. Mark has had male and female partners, but I think he has decided that he prefers men.’

‘Interesting. I hope for you that things with Johnny stay good. If not, feel free to come and cry on my shoulder.’

'Hey, *salope!*' Véronique was not happy with Juste's outrageous flirting. Sophie was used to it and laughed along as Véronique punched Juste on the arm quite hard. Juste continued once the kerfuffle had died down.

'We will soon be meeting your old friend, so we can judge for ourselves. And Henri, how are you two getting long?' Juste was smirking again, as was Véronique.

'Yes, we still get together occasionally, but I'm starting to think our little affair might have run its course. Maybe we'll just end up as friends.'

'With benefits,' Juste said. They all laughed.

Until now Sophie had not vocalised the current state of her affair with Henri or even thought about it to herself so clearly, but maybe the time had come to back off a little. She would see what happened later. She knew she wasn't in love with him, but she did find him physically attractive. She also knew that he wasn't in love with her, and she found it hard to decide if that made him more or less appealing. The affair had only really started in the first place when she had found out about Johnny and Mark; there had always been an element of revenge to it. She realised that what she wanted was for Henri to desire her, but that was receding. She would check if this had changed later. Their limited time alone together was highly charged, but was that enough? She looked at Juste and Véronique chattering away. For some reason an image of Tracey Emin's tent entered her head again, with that same feeling of connection, of sisterhood. They were both so authentic, each in their own idiosyncratic way. She had always felt that, despite everything, Johnny was authentic, but was Henri? If she was honest with herself, she thought that the answer might be no. Maybe she had punished Johnny enough.

***

Henri had arrived at the Buddha-Bar early to make sure that the table was right for the evening. He was going to sit the girls on one side of the table – he would be opposite Sophie – and Mark and Arthur would be to his left, opposite Juste and Véronique. He felt that he had neglected Sophie a little on this trip. She would be leaving tomorrow, so if they were going to sleep together it would need to be tonight. He was still keen to do so, but he had found out that she was staying with Juste and Véronique. A deliberate snub or just an invitation she hadn't been able to turn down? He would need to work hard to achieve his objective. He would try to make her feel like she was the focus of his attention this evening.

The meeting this afternoon had gone well. He had agreed a deal with Mark and Arthur; he just had to convince Caroline that it was the right thing to do. Some of Arthur's ideas on the new direction for his art were a little bit out there. He wondered if Caroline would go for them. Despite her potential misgivings, he had managed to secure what he thought was a pretty good percentage for both him and Caroline. Mark in business was not quite the pushover that he was at the poker table, and Henri was pleased that he had started with a big number in the negotiations. He had given up what appeared to be a lot of ground to Mark, but the high starting point had left him with plenty of commission to offer Caroline, even after he had taken his own cut. He hoped that the opportunity to make more commission than normal would encourage her to take more risk on the content of the art.

His Kronenbourg 1664 arrived. He wanted a quick beer, just to quench his thirst and mellow out a little in the few minutes before the others arrived. He took in the Buddha-Bar, a recent favourite venue of his for a relaxed dinner. A smart, young-looking crowd was starting to arrive, some straight from the office, the men in suits but without ties, and the women in skirts and silk blouses; later a groovier clientele would start to come in with a much more relaxed clothes vibe. The bar was known for its music, a lounge style that started as background music at a relatively low volume, gradually cranking up to a clubbier feel as the evening wore on. He lit up a Disque Bleu and inhaled deeply. He liked evenings like this; business was over, just the company of his friends to enjoy and a beautiful woman to chase. He had toyed with the idea of inviting Caroline to the dinner, but he had not wanted her to meet Arthur yet. It was better that he had sorted out a deal before he introduced her. She would want to see all the art in advance, so the first meeting would probably be in London. Soon, he hoped. Then an exhibition next year. Maybe in the spring. He found himself thinking of Caroline frequently since they had become reacquainted in Geneva. It was not just to do a business deal either. He was very keen to impress her generally; she would be a real catch. She was beautiful and highly connected, an almost perfect combination. He would play the long game with her. Tonight he would concentrate on Sophie.

***

Mark was a little nervous, something not helped by the look they were given by the security guards on the way into the Buddha-Bar. Fortunately they did not attempt to stop and search them, as Mark knew that Arthur would not have taken kindly to that. Things improved when Mark announced them to the hostess, who had been well trained in how to make people's guests feel important. She led them to the table through a large, temple-like room with a huge buddha at one end. It was a very 'Henri'-style place, Mark thought. His own immediate thought was how impractical the low lighting was, but he reminded himself that he was trying to open his eyes to new things.

'Fuck me, this is swanky.' Arthur seemed to be enjoying the vibe, however. 'Who's paying?'

'I imagine Henri will pay. He usually does. It's probably his bank paying.'

Mark hoped Arthur didn't bring this up again as they approached the table and Henri rose to greet them. Just as they were sitting down, the three women arrived. Mark made a real effort to greet Sophie warmly. He had now admitted to himself that there had been an element of revenge in the physical relationship he had with Johnny. After all, Sophie had rejected him then gone off with his best friend. This had mellowed a little with time however, and he had to say that since he had met Arthur he'd barely thought of Johnny. In this frame of mind, he realised it was much easier to try to rekindle his friendship with Sophie.

As he kissed Juste then Véronique on each cheek, he congratulated himself on how he seemed to have slipped into French greeting culture. Arthur had definitely helped his confidence. Arthur himself was his own man; he seemed to care little about what others thought of him, although Mark had realised this was only true up to a point. He cared deeply about his art and what others thought of it. In particular, the opinions of those in the art world mattered to him enormously; a negative review could crush him, even if it was in among a load of positive reviews. He watched as Arthur chatted with the two French women. They were a striking-looking couple – and it was immediately obvious that they were a couple. They sat close together; their hands entwined. Mark had never really been part of the gay scene, but he knew that a lot of queer men were quite derogatory when discussing queer women. Gay men, he had noticed, seemed to prefer straight women and often formed friendships with them. Ironically, gay women seemed to be regarded by gay men with suspicion. Despite having had relationships with and crushes on women, he had only found something deeper in his relationships with men. He found them easier to understand, for a start, less complicated. He had never quite worked women out, and queer women were an unknown quantity to him. Despite this, he would try to get to know Juste and Véronique with an open mind.

Juste was lean and striking looking. Mark found her short blonde hair and dark make-up quite severe, and it certainly had an intimidating effect. Véronique was very pretty, with a coquettish manner, less obviously queer than Juste. Arthur seemed to be in a chatty mood and was engaging them both, although Juste's English was evidently better than Véronique's, who seemed to Mark just to be nodding along. Arthur was quite temperamental generally, and the state of his mood was largely linked to his art, Mark had noticed. The success of their meeting earlier had clearly put him in a good frame of mind. Mark believed that he had negotiated a good deal; he had pushed Henri harder than he might have done previously, buoyed up by the fact that he had Arthur's backing. It was nice to be trusted in that way.

'I'm from the frozen north. You won't have been there, and you won't have heard of it, but I'm from a place called Scunthorpe.'

'No, I have not heard of it, but at least you have somewhere that you can call home. I'm a poor immigrant form the frozen east. I think more frozen than your Cunthorpe.'

Arthur and Mark smiled.

'Scunthorpe,' said Arthur, stressing the S. 'Where is it that you're from?'

'Russia. But I grew up in Paris. My father's family were Russian immigrants. He's dead now, sadly, and my mother might as well be.'

'None of us chooses our parents or our place of birth. To me these things are of little importance. What's important is what we do with our lives!'

At this, Juste offered her glass of champagne to be clinked by Arthur, who duly clinked, joined by Mark and Véronique. Henri and Sophie seemed to be deep in conversation, but Mark was too far away to hear them. Despite everything, it still hurt him to think that they still might be in a relationship. A hint of jealousy perhaps, but largely a feeling of loyalty to his friend Johnny. He knew this was hypocritical, but he felt it nonetheless. God, things were complicated!

***

'So why didn't you tell me on the phone that Mark was going to be here?' Sophie was several glasses of champagne in now and could no longer be bothered to hide her feelings from Henri. The music was getting louder, so she was having to move her head closer to Henri's.

'Careful, *mon amour*, he's going to hear you.'

She turned towards Mark at the other end of the table. They all seemed to be having a jolly time, apart from her and Henri.

'I'm sure he can't hear me. He doesn't look bothered, does he?'

'I'm sorry, I should have thought harder about it. I was under the impression that you had made up with Mark at *Sensation*.'

'I despise him a little less than I did a few years ago, but he's not my favourite person. I thought that would be obvious. I put a brave face on it most of the time, for the sake of my marriage as much as anything.'

'How is your husband, by the way? Is he still snorting his career up his nose?'

'That's not fair, Henri. And no, he is not. He's actually writing music at the moment. And spending time looking for his father. Things are good between us.' There was normally a tacit agreement between them that they did not discuss Johnny. If they did, Sophie felt that she alone had the right to slag him off. Henri did not. She knew that she could not occupy any moral high ground, but that was the way she felt. Henri just made it easy to stick to the original plan of staying at Juste and Véronique's apartment that night.

She turned away from Henri and raised her glass to the others. There was a time when she would have liked the fact that Henri had seated her opposite him and focused all his attention on her, but tonight it just seemed a little obvious on his part. Previously she had enjoyed being the centre of his attention; now she felt more like prey to his predatory instincts. Maybe it was his lack of empathy over the Mark thing, maybe she had gradually warmed back up to Johnny; whatever it was, she had the feeling that Henri may have lost his lustre. She tuned into the music; it was a very mellow vibe, nothing she had heard before. It sounded Indian, a sitar maybe. She would listen to the music, drink some champagne and have some fun with the girls.

***

Henri poured himself an Armagnac and pressed play on his CD player. The soft opening bars of 'So What' enveloped him as he sank into the sofa and lit a cigarette. He always found Miles Davis soothing at the end of an evening. He was alone at his flat in Montmartre, so things hadn't quite gone to his original plan. Ideally, the last drink of the evening would have been drunk with Sophie before they adjourned next door to his bedroom. *Tant pis*, he thought, sometimes as one door closes another one opens. He pictured himself moving smoothly and stealthily through the water, a lone shark on the hunt. His new prey was still some way off, and he would need all his charm and cunning to reel her in. Securing the contract with Arthur had been another step completed. He could tell that, despite his anti-capitalist appearance, Arthur liked money. Most people from humble backgrounds did. Henri had also observed how Arthur behaved at the bank where they had had the meeting, then at the Buddha-Bar; while he outwardly affected an indifference to the elevated surroundings, his body language betrayed him. Arthur liked the trappings of wealth and the lifestyle that went with it. This was a good thing, as it meant that he was incentivised to make money. Henri could also tell that he was serious about his art, but what he wanted more than anything was success. The art would be influenced by that underlying ambition. For Henri, this combination was perfect. He would be difficult to manage, but Mark could help him with that. Mark had definitely fallen under Arthur's spell. They way that he looked at him with wide eyes it was clear that they were lovers already. All of this was good for Henri; it moved him closer to Caroline and closer to the world of contemporary art. His job at the bank paid the rent, but the world he was entering had way more potential. It was strange that a scruffy, wild-eyed artist from Scunthorpe was the key.

***

'Just one more little glass of champagne, surely.'

Sophie was drunk, as were Juste and Véronique, but Juste wanted another drink.

'No, baby, I'm going to bed,' Véronique tottered off to their bedroom leaving Sophie and Juste to finish the champagne. If she was worried about Juste flirting with Sophie, then she was too tired and too pissed to care.

Their apartment was close enough to Henri's that he had dropped them off in the car that he had organised. The *trois-pièces* was close to where the girls had their shop on the Clignancourt side of Montmartre. Sophie had been there before but had never stayed over. She watched as Juste poured out the rest of the bottle of Lanson Black Label. They were sitting close to each other on the sofa in what was a chic salon, decorated in a contemporary style influenced by art deco. Black-lacquered furniture, mirrors and leopard skin featured heavily. It was a proper boudoir.

'So that was a lovely evening.' Juste had begun to speak English. She put her arm around Sophie's shoulders as she sat back. Sophie felt relaxed enough to lean her head on Juste's shoulder. Her mind was a little fuzzy, but she recognised a hint of sexual frisson in the apparently innocent gesture.

'Have you ever been kissed by a woman?' Juste said softly.

'No,' she replied.

'Would you like to try?' Juste was being most unlike her

normal brash self. Her manner felt soft and gentle, but with an undercurrent of authority. Sophie turned her mouth to meet Juste, who kissed her, tenderly at first then more firmly. Sophie was immediately aroused by her, and she felt herself kissing Juste back, her lips tingling as she did. Something in her brain, however, was telling her that it was a bad idea, her body language must have communicated this to Juste, who broke away from her.

'What's wrong?' she asked. 'I hope you don't feel guilty after the things that your pig of a husband has done.'

'No, it's not Johnny, it's Véronique,' Sophie said quietly.

'She knows I stray. It doesn't mean that I am any less in love with her. In fact, it's the reverse; it makes us stronger.'

'That's very French, Juste, but I don't think I'm built like that. It's not that I didn't like kissing you, I did, I really did, but I don't think I can do it to Véronique. I think it breaks some kind of sisterly code.'

'Well, that's not a code that I'm familiar with.' Juste looked her in the eyes and stroked her cheek. Sophie shivered a little. 'If you change your mind, you know where I am.'

Sophie felt very drawn to her gaze and her touch, but something was holding her back. She moved forward and pressed her lips to Juste's for a final kiss. Juste's mouth felt smaller and softer than a man's. The sensation of kissing was different; it was gentler, somehow more emotional. She definitely liked it very much, and she liked Juste very much, but this was not the right time or place.

'Thanks for being understanding,' she said, touching the back of her neck, the cropped hairs softer than she expected.

Juste smiled a knowing smile. 'Time for bed,' she said. 'You are in that one.' She pointed at the door opposite the one that Véronique had disappeared into a few minutes earlier. 'Sleep well, my darling,' Juste whispered in her ear.

THE NARCISSIST

MARCH 1998

Sophie was woken by Johnny snuggling into her. She could feel in the small of her back that he was hard. She knew it was early as Amy had not yet woken them. The vague images of an erotic dream were coming back to her, but who was it in the dream? She still felt a little horny and she pushed herself against Johnny, responding to his own state of arousal. He began to touch her body gently; she still enjoyed his touch, which was firm but gentle, almost feminine. She drifted back to half sleep as Johnny touched her; the dream was coming back to her, it was Juste. They were on the sofa at the apartment in Paris where they had kissed briefly after the night at the Buddha-Bar. Johnny was physically stronger than Juste, but their wiry bodies were similar in a way. She felt herself turning Johnny on to his back and mounting him. She closed her eyes as images in her mind of Juste and Johnny blurred into one.

When they had finished she laid her head on Johnny's shoulder. She felt the relaxed feeling of post-coital sexual satisfaction; she hoped Johnny felt the same but could not bring herself to ask him directly. It was strange how you could be so physically close to someone and yet not discuss it. She thought this was probably her issue rather than Johnny's; it was such a difficult thing to ask your partner to comment on your sexual performance. Better to wait for them to tell you. They lay silently for a few minutes as their breathing gradually levelled out.

'So, I think I'm going to try to see him,' Johnny said finally, breaking the silence.

'Who?'

'My dad, of course. Marty. I just need to go and see my mum and talk it through with her.'

'Have you mentioned wanting to find him? We only seem to talk about Amy when I see her.'

'No, I haven't said anything. It's such a tough subject to broach. She hates talking about him. Gran said she would speak to her now that she's let the cat out of the bag, but I know she hasn't. That was months ago.'

'I know it means a lot to you to have found him.'

'Yeah, it does. But, now that I have, I'm really unsure about how to handle it. Strange that he's not in Brighton at all. Hackney of all places. It's really not somewhere that I would have started looking.'

'Are you definitely sure its him.'

'Well, I'm pretty certain. Funny that he's a jobbing musician. I don't suppose I'd have found him otherwise. Martin Brown is such a common name. He was just about well enough known in musical circles in the end. Someone described him as being an old-school axeman. No one has ever connected us because I'm Johnny Jones and he's Marty Brown.'

'Axe as in guitar, I take it?' She felt Johnny smiling.

'Yeah, that term has rather dated now, hasn't it? He seems to live on his own. I've got a phone number. I'm just going to have to ring it and see what happens. Apparently he dabbles in art, too, so I've heard on the grapevine.'

Sophie squeezed Johnny. The issue of his dad had been bothering him for months now. She would like him to be at peace with it. She was convinced that his missing father was at the root of his issues with booze and cocaine.

Sophie heard the door handle start to move. Her daughter's face appeared around the door.

'Mum, I need my PE kit today.'

'OK, darling. Good morning, by the way.'

'Good morning, Mummy. And Daddy.'

Just like that she was gone. Amy loved school, everything about it. It did mean she took it all very seriously, so woe betide Sophie if she forgot Amy's PE kit. She glanced at the clock by the bed. It was only seven. They still had some time before they had to get up. Often the bedroom was the only place where they had a proper conversation.

'Have you decided if you're coming to Paris for Arthur's exhibition?'

'When is it again?'

'It's in a couple of weeks. I'm definitely going. I'll go and see Juste and Véronique at the same time. They'll probably come to the exhibition, too. We can stay with them if you like?'

'If I come, I'd rather stay in a hotel, I think. To be honest, I'm in two minds. I'm a bit pissed off with Mark and Arthur. I can't get over the fact that Arthur is gay. I didn't even have an inkling. That big, hairy wanker. I hardly hear from Mark these days, or Arthur for that matter.'

Since it had become obvious that Mark and Arthur were a couple, Sophie had noticed that Johnny became irritated when their names came up. He was clearly a little jealous of the relationship. Sophie couldn't work out what kind of jealous this was; jilted like a best friend or jilted like a lover. She tried to concentrate on it being the former, but it was difficult to block out thoughts of the latter.

'I think there's a lot more to Arthur than his being big and hairy. I don't find him attractive, but I can see how someone would. He exudes confidence for a start; he's very self-assured, intelligent and a successful artist.'

'Mark knows nothing about art. He's a cultural void.'

'I think he's trying. We talked about *Sensation* when I saw him in Paris. He was talking about the Chapman Brothers' mannequins, how they had really made him think – with Arthur's help, of course.'

'What a faker. He's just interested in Arthur as a client. He doesn't give a shit about art.'

'I don't think so, Johnny. Anyway, if you come to the Paris exhibition you can find out.'

'I'll think about it. Thanks for understanding. I know Mark's not your best mate these days, so it's good of you to be standing up for him.'

Why was she standing up for him? She felt much less threatened by Mark now that he was with Arthur, she realised. And he was Johnny's best friend; in a peculiar way, she didn't want Johnny to lose the friendship, as long as it was that and nothing more.

'Well, I *have* known him a long time, and he *is* your best friend.'

'Best friend that I never see.'

'Well maybe you should reach out.'

'I have got that acoustic gig coming up in Islington next week. Maybe I'll give Mark a ticket for that. He used to be my biggest fan, but I'm not sure he even knows that the gig is happening. I told you we're keeping it hush-hush to try and create a bit of hype.'

'You should definitely invite him, and Arthur.'

'I'm not sure about Arthur.'

'They're a couple, Mark.'

'I suppose so.'

'Do you want me to come to the gig, by the way? I can ask my mum to look after Amy, or she can go to your mum?'

'That's a nice thought. Have a think about it. I know you've got a lot on with Amy and the shop and everything, but it might be fun. Like the old days.'

She smiled. The old days. They were only just into their thirties, but a lot had happened in a short space of time.

'Up to you, babe.'

Johnny certainly wasn't controlling in any way, shape or form. If she wanted to do something, she did it, and he normally backed her up. At times she wished he cared more. He had never challenged her when he had found out about Henri. It had been overshadowed at the time by him and Mark being outed, but she had still cheated on her husband, and he had hardly reacted to that. In some ways it was good that he was forgiving, but if that forgiveness was just a front for not really caring, then it was not so great. She knew that feeling like this was hypocritical, but that was how it was.

'You won't forget about the PE kit, will you, Mum.'

Reluctantly Sophie rose from her bed. It seemed that the day had started.

***

'So did you like Swerve back in the day?'

Arthur took a sip of his pint of bitter before he answered. They were in the Baring Arms at the bottom of Southgate Road, near the canal. It was almost equidistant for each of them to walk to, Mark from his flat in Highbury and Arthur from his studio just off Brick Lane. The Baring was an old-school boozer in an area that still had just about enough old-school customers to keep it going. For how much longer, Mark was not sure, but for the moment, they both enjoyed meeting at this quiet little Victorian establishment. It provided anonymity and neutral ground to chat in. The pubs near Arthur tended to be full of his fellow artists, and, much as Arthur seemed to enjoy the camaraderie of his peers, Mark knew that he liked to take a break from them, too.

'It's not that far back, is it? They only split up a year or two ago, didn't they?'

'Well, I always think of Swerve as the classic line-up with Johnny on guitar, Alex Middlehead on vocals, Dave Simpson on bass and Rob Baldini on drums. That finished for me when Johnny left after the second album.'

'They were always a bit too fuckin' trite for me. 'Lost in Space'. Where's their self-respect, for fuck's sake?'

'I think Alex was the more commercially minded of the band. That poppy stuff was more him. Johnny was always more influenced by some of the stuff that you're quite into, like the New York Dolls, the Stooges, punk, that kind of thing.'

'OK, if you insist. Why do you ask?' Arthur was always straight to the point.

'Well, I haven't seen much of Johnny recently, but he's just been in touch. He's doing a gig up the road at the Powerhaus. It's a kind of Nirvana Unplugged, if you like. Some new songs, some old songs, in an acoustic set with Dave and Rob on bass and drums. I think it'll be great.'

'Well, you're his biggest fan, so you would do.' Mark coloured a little. Arthur continued, 'You manage my diary anyway, so let's put it in. When is it?'

'Next week. Just a few days before you're due in Paris. Is everything on track for that?'

Arthur didn't like Mark going to the studio, so he hadn't seen the art that Arthur was planning to take. However, he knew that Caroline Schmidt was going to approve it, so that made him less anxious.

'It'll blow your fuckin' socks off.' Arthur laughed his hearty laugh. Mark followed with a more nervous titter.

'Are you sure you still don't want to tell me what the surprise piece is?'

'As I've told you, my dear, the only person who's going to know that is me. All will be revealed when the curtain is drawn back.'

'What will Caroline and Henri say when you tell them there is a surprise piece? You have remembered that they're going to be at the studio tomorrow afternoon for the final approval of the art?'

'Well, I just won't tell them. And, yes, of course I've remembered.'

'Seriously?'

'It's a surprise. If I tell them, it won't be a surprise. I'm shipping the piece in a box under instruction that only I am allowed to open it, and even then behind a curtain immediately before the exhibition starts.'

'Any chance of a clue?'

'It's very personal.'

'That's it?'

'That's all you're getting, pal.'

Arthur had not been joking when he had told Mark that he would not be involved in artistic decisions. He felt a little uncomfortable being frozen out like this, but he had learned that confronting Arthur with negativity was the wrong approach. He knew he would worry now about Arthur's potential to do something outlandish, but he would just have to accept that. Their relationship was more complicated than it might initially have appeared; the closer he felt he was getting to Arthur, the more he felt Arthur pushed him away a little.

***

Henri became more and more uncomfortable as the taxi drove further from the City into the hinterland to the east. He had dressed down a little for the visit to Arthur's studio, but when he had met Caroline at Gare du Nord he realised that he had forgotten to mention clothing to her. He wore a pair of black Levi's, a grey cashmere roll-neck jumper by Gucci and a black leather coat, also by Gucci. He was hoping that the look would work in the City as well as on the fringes of it. Caroline was dressed more for Mayfair than Shoreditch. For starters, she was wearing a Cartier tank watch in gold with a gold strap. This alone, Henri knew, was worth nearly the annual salary of some of the local residents. She looked extremely elegant, as she always did; Henri was just concerned that they would be mugged. He figured that he would make sure that the black cab stopped very close to the door of the studio.

This was in a disused warehouse behind Rivington Street. Henri always carried a copy of the *London A–Z* streetmap on his trips to London, and he could see where they were and where they needed to go. Caroline was talking on her mobile to a client, oblivious to his concerns. Living in Geneva could make you complacent about the safety of big cities, but Henri had spent enough time in Paris and London to understand that looking out of place at the wrong time among the wrong people was not a great idea.

He had hoped that their trip to London would include an overnight stay, but Caroline's relentless schedule had not allowed it; this meant they were on a one-day Eurostar Paris–London return. In the end they had cut it too fine with the visit in any case, as it had effectively become too late to cancel the Paris show, even if Caroline did not like what she saw at Arthur's studio. It would be happening in less than two weeks, and invitations had already been sent. The numbers responding positively were significant, confirming Henri's view that they were riding some kind of wave, or *nouvelle vague*, as Caroline might say.

They pulled up next to an alleyway off Rivington Street.

'I think it's down there, mate,' said their cabby. Henri could see in the mirror that his expression was questioning exactly what two well-dressed Parisians were doing in an alley in Shoreditch, but, unusually, he was too polite to ask.

'I have to go,' said Caroline, finishing her call.

Henri got out first then offered his hand to help her from the cab, an offer she accepted with a smile. 'It's nice to spend some time with a gentleman, Henri,' she said. 'There aren't very many in the art world. I don't remember you being this polite at school.'

'No, you're probably right there.' Henri was pretty sure he had been too much in awe of her to behave badly towards her at school. He hoped she was just teasing him.

Once he had paid the cab, he motioned protectively with his arm for her to go in front and hustled her a little way down the alley to the entrance to the studio. Mark had explained that there was no bell; they should just let themselves in. Mark himself would not be there; Arthur would show them around. He was pretty sure they were in the right place as he could hear what sounded like the Velvet Underground playing loudly on the other side of the wall.

Henri opened the door, and they walked into a large room, where the music was now at jet-engine-decibel level. At one end of the room a man in a leather apron and welding helmet was at work on a piece of metal. The dark hair sprouting from the headgear gave away his identity. Henri left Caroline standing by the door and picked his way through the accumulated detritus that covered the floor towards Arthur, who still had no idea that they had walked in. Once he got near him, he gesticulated, hoping to attract his attention before he fired up the welder again and destroyed Henri's eyesight. Arthur put down the piece of metal he was holding and waved at him, grinning. He walked over to an old fifties-looking sideboard in the corner of the room that had a turntable on it and lifted the stylus from the vinyl LP that was playing. Suddenly there was silence.

'Now then, Monsieur le Cerf, a pleasure to see you,' he said from a distance of a few yards, wiping his hands on an oily rag that looked as if it would be adding oil to his hands rather than removing it.

'And this must be Madame Schmidt. Welcome to my humble abode.'

'Thank you, Mr Swale. It's fascinating to see the artist in his atelier.'

'Is that a posh word for studio?' asked Arthur. 'Please call me Arthur, by the way.'

'No, I think it's just a French word. I thought it was used in English, too.'

'Only joshing,' said Arthur making his way over to Caroline. It took a while for him to negotiate the pieces of metal, wood, tools and metalworking machines that littered the floor. Henri realised, as he watched Arthur and Caroline shake hands, that there were a number of items at the other end of the room covered in sheets. He guessed these were the works for the exhibition. Against the longest wall of the studio were floor-to-ceiling racks of shelving that housed large quantities of all sorts of metal. Some looked as if they were new, piles of reinforcing steel normally used for concrete, piles of steel with holes in it, what looked like other metals, too, aluminium maybe in sheets, as well as all sorts of random pieces of metal and plastic that had clear marks of previous use and might normally be in a scrapyard or a skip. It was quite a hoard.

'Over here, Henri lad,' called Arthur. He was removing a sheet that covered the larger of the items at the other end of the room. Henri moved to join them to take a closer look.

'You've seen this one before, Henri, but not this close up. And I think you've seen a photo, Caroline.'

It was *The Narcissist.* Arthur found a switch hidden inside the framework of the sculpture, which started the pump enabling the effect of the narcissist peeing into his own mouth, simultaneously grotesque and funny, thought Henri, but probably just grotesque to some. He waited for Caroline's reaction. She started to laugh.

'This is ingenious. It looks so much better than in the photo,' she said, walking around the piece to take it all in. 'How does it work from a practical point of view.'

'Where my pieces are motorised, it's with a mechanism that can be wound up normally with a key, a bit like a clock or like an automaton. These can be wound when the piece is not being displayed. Technology allows them to last quite a while now with one winding. I'm working on new technologies that give even more power, too. It's interesting that you ask. Most people aren't curious enough to find out how my stuff works. You must have an enquiring mind.'

'I'm thinking about the practicalities of selling the art. That sounds quite straightforward. As long as they don't go wrong.'

'Well, as you know, Mr Saatchi owns this piece, and I believe he's been very happy with it. As far as selling it, in my experience, he's always open to offers, so I think you can assume that this is for sale for the purposes of our exhibition but by negotiation with Mr Saatchi only. It was good of him to lend it to us, to be honest. He didn't have to. These are the ones that are definitely for sale through you.' Arthur gestured to the other works then walked around them removing all the sheets with a flourish. 'These are *The Seven Deadly Sins*,' he announced. In previous conversations Arthur had been mysterious about exactly what would be exhibited, saying only that the pieces were in the style of *The Narcissist*. As he revealed the central pieces to the new exhibition, Henri was genuinely taken aback. Arthur walked around each one turning the switches on, and the seven sins jumped into life.

'Wow, *mais c'est incroyable*.' Caroline was clearly impressed.

Henri moved closer for a better look. Immediately in front of him there were two large, motorised rabbits fornicating. It looked as if they were metal-framed models covered in rabbit skins. The one behind, presumably the male, had the word LUST stamped on his back in red letters. Every couple of minutes the male rabbit let out a squeal. Henri moved on to the next of the machines, which was a model of a large human head wearing a straw boater, with large, mad eyes and ruddy cheeks. This gentleman had an Edwardian look and wore a stiff collar and a bow tie that had the word WRATH embroidered into it in capitals. Henri realised that the overall look was that of an oversized ventriloquist's dummy. As he moved closer, suddenly the head let out a large scream, the boater sprang up in the air, the eyes popped out and the mouth opened to reveal a large, bright-red tongue. Genuinely quite disturbing, in a sixties-horror-film style. Not frightening, disturbing.

He looked over at Caroline, whom he hadn't realised was in deep conversation with Arthur next to a piece that looked as if it was made of green oxidised copper. It had the appearance of a green-eyed *Tyrannosaurus rex*, Henri realised. Of course, the green-eyed monster. Sure enough, as he walked over he could make out ENVY in copper lettering on the chest of the monster. It was a fearsome-looking thing, at least eight feet tall, it's head and body moving backwards and forwards on a fixed framework of legs. The penny was starting to drop with Henri. These were modern automata, not only in the way that they worked but in the ingenious way that they were designed. He had rarely seen Caroline so animated in conversation.

'These are wonderful, Arthur,' she repeated as she walked around each of the exhibits in turn.'

Things were moving in the right direction.

***

On the train back to Paris, Caroline was full of enthusiasm for what she had seen.

'I don't mind telling you, Henri, I was a little nervous about this trip. I trust you, but I know you're not an art expert. I'm the art expert, and I knew I was taking a risk. My parents were not too keen and have taken some persuading, I can tell you. But I will be proud to put on this exhibition. Arthur has such a creative mind, and the detail and workmanship in the manufacture of the pieces is truly astonishing. He's such a product of the industrial north of England. It's all so persuasive. I have no doubt the pieces will sell, maybe to one collector. Wouldn't it be great if the collection stayed together?'

Henri agreed with Caroline and let her continue talking in the same vein. It was wonderful to see her so upbeat. He studied her as she spoke. He realised that there was something of the late Princess of Wales in the way that Caroline looked. She was tall and athletic looking, maybe a little fuller figured than the princess and not quite as striking, but there was a similarity. She had the same vivacious sparkle in her eye when she talked about something that pleased her. Now that he knew her a little better, he sensed that she also masked a vulnerability that she and Diana also shared. It had been such a shock when Diana had died last year. Henri realised that it was the coexistence of toughness and vulnerability in her personality that he found so attractive. In Emily there was too much vulnerability, in Sophie maybe not enough, but in Caroline maybe the right balance. He let her carry on talking.

'I think I might even have someone for the whole collection. Vladimir in New York. He loves contemporary art, I know he has works by Basquiat, Jeff Koons and Keith Haring to name a few. I wonder if I can tempt him over for the exhibition. He hasn't replied to my invitation yet.'

'I'm sure he won't be able to resist your charms if you call him.'

There was a hint of a smile as she replied, 'Yes, I must.'

She continued to talk about the exhibition, the invitation list, ideas for exactly how it might be displayed to best effect, about Arthur, asking Henri what more he knew about him. Henri remained calm in his responses; he was playing the long game with Caroline. She was his ticket to a world that he was desperate to enter. It was a world of the mega-rich, the ultra-high-net-worth individuals, HNWIs for short. These clients were the holy grail for the private banker, but Henri could now glimpse a future beyond banking. Caroline's introductions would allow him to become independently wealthy. He would no longer be the adviser; he would be the client. That was the biggest attraction of all.

***

Johnny always felt nervous before a gig. It was worse these days, as he kept pretty clean before playing. He'd had a couple of Jack Daniels and a cleansing ale to follow, but it wasn't enough to rid him of the nerves. He was in the small dressing-room with his old

Swerve mates Dave and Rob. As usual Dave was having a nap in one corner, and Rob was pacing the room. They were like chalk and cheese before a gig, Dave so laid back that he was actually asleep, and Rob like a coiled spring, ready to unleash himself on his drum kit. At least he only had brushes rather than drumsticks to practise with on the small Formica table provided to them. They were going to go for a mellow vibe tonight: acoustic guitar for Johnny, acoustic bass for Dave and brushes and a pared-down kit for Rob. Johnny felt as if they had rehearsed enough, but it still felt weird that their old lead singer and self-appointed leader of the band Alex wasn't around. Johnny blamed Alex for forcing him out of Swerve, but now that Swerve had recently imploded, and several years had passed since Alex had manoeuvred him out, he had stopped the hating. He wondered if Alex felt the same; maybe not, given that Dave and Rob had publicly joined Johnny for this gig. Even so, they had put Alex on the guest list, and Rob had called to let him know, but no one had heard back from him. Swerve's recent final split, long after Johnny had left, had finally drawn a line under that whole period: the band's rapid rise to fame and its even quicker fall had impacted him in so many ways, not least the temporary break-up of his marriage. But that was all behind him now; he felt more positive about his music than he had since Alex had kicked him out. He had collaborated on a few recordings in the meantime – in truth, as little more than a session guitarist – but this latest clutch of what were largely his own songs was the first time that he had had the courage to get out there again and put his name and reputation on the line. He was singing on his own live tonight for the first time. This was a much bigger deal than the backing vocals he had always sung with Swerve. He was confident that his voice would stand up, but he was nervous of the comparisons that would be drawn with Alex. Some of the music press would be here tonight – he had called in a few favours to make that happen – and he knew that the people coming were pretty hardnosed, tough to impress.

He tuned into the music they had playing in the background in the dressing-room and tried to think forward not backwards. Kurt Cobain's voice intoned the words of one of his favourites on the *Nirvana Unplugged* album, 'On a Plain'. He preferred the acoustic version to the original track; it just suited the treatment so well, he thought. He had tried to channel the feel of this album into their rehearsals, and it had gone pretty well. It was a small but influential venue here at the Powerhaus; now all they needed was to pull it off in front of an important crowd, and he might be on his way again. By the time he finally met his father he wanted him to be proud, not think that he had had it all and thrown it away. He looked at the clock in the small changing-room. It was time to rally the troops. He stood up, took a sip of his can of Red Stripe, brushed down his black *Raw Power* T-shirt and lit up a Marlboro Light.

'Right, guys. Dave, wake up, dude, it's almost time to rumble.'

Dave stirred and rubbed his eyes open. 'Yes, boss.'

Even Rob managed to stop pacing and walk on the spot instead. His eager face exposed his amphetamine habit. Johnny felt the earring in his left ear, a habit that seemed to help his concentration.

'Let's give this one everything, fellas. We were super-tight in rehearsal, so we know we can do it. There are important people out there. Let's go and impress them.'

The three of them huddled together and joined hands before making the short walk down the corridor to the stage.

Johnny had wanted to keep things low key, so there was no MC to announce them. They just walked on stage quietly, took their places, Johnny seated at the front, with Dave stood behind him next to Rob and his drum kit. There was a ripple of low-key applause. He looked out towards the crowd of a couple of hundred and recognised a few faces immediately. The music-press crowd had definitely turned up. He took a long draught on his can of Red Stripe, stubbed out his Marlboro in the ashtray next to him and took the plectrum from the strings of his guitar. He had decided to open with possibly the least acoustic song he knew, 'Search and Destroy' by Iggy and the Stooges. It was tricky technically for two reasons. Firstly, he was only playing one guitar, and two guitar parts were needed to replicate the original opening. For his acoustic version he had decided to stick to the chord progression without attempting to overlay any of the searing guitar solo of the original. The second issue was hitting the vocals bang on time with sufficient impetus but without singing too loudly. This was a song with a lot of forward momentum, which was hard to maintain acoustically.

'You might know this one,' he said into the microphone by way of introduction. Then on the count of four they were away, right in sync, the chords coming easily to his fingers, backed up by Dave's melodious bass and the soft percussion of Rob's brushes. He hit the opening lines perfectly: 'I'm a streetwalkin' cheetah with a heart full of napalm / I'm a runaway son of the nuclear A-bomb.' His nerves disappeared, they were on it, he felt good, he could lose himself in the music.

Johnny had decided to play his new song 'Dead Dad' as the penultimate number. He had to finish with 'Lost in Space', Swerve's biggest hit, to please the crowd. The set so far seemed to have gone down well, with most people in the relatively small crowd nodding along and clapping enthusiastically. He felt confident about his new song as he introduced it.

'This next one was inspired by a work of art I saw not long ago. It's for all the dads out there. And all the children. Particularly those of you who don't know your father or have lost him. It's called "Dead Dad".'

He suddenly felt a lump in his throat as he began the opening chords. It was a gentle chord progression, repeated twice before the lyrics started, by which time the lump had receded and he was able to hit the opening lines.

An hour later Johnny, Dave and Rod stood at the front of the small stage at the end of the gig with their arms around one another.

They basked for a couple of minutes in the fulsome applause before jumping down from the stage to join the crowd and head to the bar. It seemed a little too exclusive to retreat to their tiny dressing-room, particularly when they knew a lot of the people in the crowd. He walked through the first clump of people who looked as if they were Swerve fans, a little younger than him, girls with long, straight hair, crop-tops and bell bottoms next to boys with longish but more tousled locks in indie T-shirts. Some of them patted him on the back as he walked through towards the bar. He then spotted Mark accompanied by Arthur. Mark was beaming at him. His expression took Johnny back to the early days of Swerve, when Mark had been a super-fan. Johnny knew that he had exploited that, particularly when he thought about the physical side of their relationship. It had started around that time, and it had always been about Mark giving him pleasure. He had never really reciprocated. He was not very proud of the way he had been, but, despite himself, he was still jealous of Arthur Swale. And there stood the great sculptor, as large as life, or possibly larger. Before he knew it Arthur was giving him a bear hug. Mark carried on grinning next to him.

'Get that man a fuckin' pint,' Arthur said, once he had put Johnny down.

Mark just patted him on the back. 'Well done, mate. I can't quite believe how good your vocals were. Seriously. It was fucking brilliant.'

Before he knew it Johnny was surrounded by well-wishers, people he knew, people he half knew, people he had never met, all telling how wonderful his performance had been. Several people offered him a drink, then three arrived at the same time. He had missed this, the adrenaline buzz of the live performance coupled with the adoration of the crowd. He would need to be careful. He had a big day tomorrow. He was staying at Mark's flat tonight, then he was making the short trip over to Hackney to knock on his father's door and introduce himself. He knew that he might have a bit of a hangover, but he wanted to keep it to a minimum. He would hang out to take the plaudits for a while, but make sure he didn't go too crazy which the high of the gig made it so easy to do.

He managed to talk Mark and Arthur into leaving after a couple more drinks, shocking himself at his self-discipline. To Johnny's further surprise, Arthur then immediately disappeared on foot in the direction of Shoreditch. He had thought that Arthur would be coming back to Mark's flat, which would at least have meant that he and Mark would not be there alone together. He now felt slightly awkward, as the sleeping arrangements had suddenly become less certain. He and Mark took the familiar walk north along Upper Street, avoiding the hustlers and drunks, to Highbury Corner, then up the eastern side of Highbury Fields to Mark's flat in a Georgian townhouse overlooking the park. Small but perfectly formed, as Mark called it. Small but large enough to have a second bedroom. Johnny had stayed with Mark occasionally since Mark's last girlfriend Victoria had moved out several years ago, and each time he had ended up in Mark's double bed rather than in the single in the small guest room. The inevitable had then ensued on each occasion. He wondered if it would happen again tonight.

Johnny slumped into the chintzy sofa in Mark's living-room and sparked up a Marlboro Light. He inhaled the first drag of smoke deeply and exhaled.

'Nightcap?' asked Mark.

'Yes please, mate. Have you got any malt whisky?'

'How about a Laphroaig.'

'Perfect.'

'It couldn't have gone much better tonight,' said Mark as he poured the drinks. 'I loved the new stuff. I think "Dead Dad" was a favourite. I remember that naked model at the exhibition. It wasn't like a sculpture, much more like a model, in colour, just a bit smaller than life size. Fortunately, mine's not dead yet. I suppose I should appreciate him more, the fucking homophobe.'

It was unlike Mark to swear, thought Johnny. But he was right, Mark's dad would never accept Mark being gay or even bisexual; he was a proper old-school homophobe.

'The power of music, eh?' he said.

'The power of art, Arthur would say. It all started with *Dead Dad* the sculpture; the music came next.'

'Talking of dead dads, I'm hoping to see mine tomorrow.'

'What, your dad? I didn't think you even knew who he was?'

'Well, his name is Marty Brown. He's a musician, and he lives in Hackney. My gran finally cracked and told me who he was, and I've been looking for him ever since. It turns out that he's also a guitarist. I found him through the musicians' grapevine. I haven't had the heart to tell my mum that I know.'

'Jesus, that's incredible, mate. After all this time! Where are you meeting him?'

'Well, I haven't sorted that out yet. I'm going to go over to Hackney, call him on my mobile and see how he reacts. If it goes well, I'll go round to his flat; if it goes badly, I'll go to the pub. Maybe I'll give you a call if it's the latter.'

Mark looked slightly uneasy when he said this. 'I've got a pretty full day tomorrow. I have an audit meeting first thing in the West End, then I'm meeting Arthur in the afternoon to go through the plans for transporting the art to Paris for the exhibition. '

'It seems like you and Arthur are pretty tight?'

'Well, yes, I suppose we are. I'd never really thought of it like that. He's quite mysterious, so we're not in each other's pockets. But, yes, we're close.'

'You've never talked to me about him.'

'Have I not?' Johnny could see that Mark was now squirming and thought he should back off. He was definitely jealous of what Mark had with Arthur, but there was no need for him to put Mark through the wringer for it. The old him might have created a scene in a drunken stupor, but he hoped he was past that.

'No worries. I'm pleased for you, mate. I really hope it works out.'

'Thanks. I appreciate that.' It looked as though Mark was not going to be any more forthcoming than that. Johnny downed the rest of his Laphroaig.

'I think I'm going to crash. Where do you want me?' he asked.

'The guest room is made up. I've left you a towel.'

'How civilised we've become,' Johnny said with a chuckle. 'I'll see you in the morning. Busy days ahead, eh?'

'Yeah. Goodnight, mate.'

An hour or so later Johnny lay alone in the guest room looking at the ceiling. He wondered if Mark might come and get into bed with him. That seemed unlikely now. He wondered if he should tap on Mark's door. He decided he wouldn't cope well with a rejection and forced his mind to let it drop. He thought of Sophie and Amy at home instead, which gave him a warmer feeling. Tonight had also been a bit of a revelation. Being on stage like that, out front, leading the band, had given him a huge buzz. He wanted more of that. If things went well with his dad tomorrow, he might finally feel like his life was back on track. Mark and he could remain friends. They had just proved that.

***

Johnny tapped the numbers in on his new mobile. Mark had gone to work so he was alone in the flat. He had just told Sophie what he was about to do, and she had encouraged him to go ahead. It was ten o'clock. He had left it quite late to call, as he figured that if Marty had been playing the night before he might be lying in. He pressed the green button on his phone, and it started to ring.

''Allo.'

Johnny spotted the South Coast twang straight away. It was the right number.

'Hello, it's Johnny here.'

'Johnny who?'

'Johnny Jones, Mary's son.'

'Mary who?'

This was like pulling teeth.

'Mary Jones. My mother.'

'Right, gotcha.'

'I think you might be my dad.'

There was a long pause.

'Right.'

'I was born in Hastings on June the 9th 1967.'

'Right.'

'Does that ring any bells?'

Johnny was tiring of the monosyllabic replies.

'A mate of mine mentioned that you were looking for me. I know who you are.'

'So, do you think you're my dad?'

'Well, if you're Mary's boy, I probably am.'

'Probably.'

'Yeah, probably.'

Johnny let it pass.

'How would you feel about meeting up.'

'Well, I don't know. I haven't had much time to think about it.'

Johnny would have preferred a bit more enthusiasm.

'How about some breakfast now?'

'Well, you've kind of got me on the hop . . .' His father's voice trailed off.

'Look, I'm in Highbury. I know you're not far away. What have we got to lose?'

There was another long pause.

'There's a greasy spoon in Ridley Road, Dalston. It's the Kingsland Road end, where the market is. It's called the Market Café. I'll meet you there in an hour.'

'OK. No problem.'

'And, Johnny, thanks for getting in touch.'

The phone went dead at the other end. Marty was obviously a little thrown by the call, although the fact that he had thanked him at the end was encouraging.

Forty-five minutes later Johnny had picked his way through the bustle of Ridley Road market and was in the Market Café sucking on a Marlboro Light and sipping on chipped mug of builder-strength tea. He didn't know Dalston that well, but there seemed to be a diverse group of punters in the caff; the owner and staff looked Greek or Turkish, there was a sprinkling of older Caribbean-looking guys, joshing and cackling, a few less-chirpy-looking older white guys in cloth caps and sheepskins and an eclectic collection of younger-looking studenty types of all hues sporting a mixture of different vintage-shop garbs. The tables and chairs were fifties or sixties blond wood and Formica. The kitchen at one end of the room behind a counter was the source of loud shouts each time a plate or two of fried food was ready. This was delivered at regular intervals by the young waitresses clad in maroon Nylon house-coats. There was a general hubbub in the room, accompanied by clouds of cigarette smoke and steam rising from the mugs and plates of hot food. It was the time of day when most people were at work, thought Johnny wryly, other than people like him and his dad, who had chosen a different path. Before he had time to reflect any further, a tall, lean figure slipped into the seat opposite him and immediately lit a cigarette.

'I see we have the same bad habits,' Marty said with a smile, blowing out a cloud of smoke.

Johnny smiled back at him. 'I was wondering how I would recognise you,' he said, 'but it seems I don't need to worry about that.'

'I spotted you straight away. You favour your mother. That's as clear as day.'

While this was true, Johnny could also see himself in his father immediately; there was something about the way he took a drag on his cigarette, talked as he blew the smoke out then smiled that he recognised in himself. He had decided to tread carefully at the first meeting, as he didn't want it to be the last, particularly given the degree to which Marty had held back when they had spoken on the phone. He planned to try to save most of the hundreds of questions he had for future occasions.

The waitress approached and greeted Marty by name. He was obviously a regular.

'My usual please, Daphne.'

'So that's the full English with no beans.'

'Yes please. And what do you want Johnny?' Marty asked him.

'I'll have the same,' said Johnny. 'I don't like beans with a breakfast either. They ruin it.'

'Exactly my view, too,' said Marty. They grinned at each other.

The waitress fixed her eyes on Johnny briefly. 'Do I know you?' she asked.

'No, I don't think so,' he said. 'I'm Johnny. Marty's son.' It sounded very strange saying it.

'Really? I didn't know you 'ad a son, Marty. All these years comin' in 'ere and not a mention.'

'Well, I don't like to brag.' He smiled at Johnny again. Daphne moved away with their orders, and Johnny noticed Marty's eyes follow her walk back to the counter. The roving eye spotted first hand.

'The Greek girls who serve in here are all lovely,' Marty said, by way of confirmation. 'Lovely country Greece.' Johnny wondered if he might elaborate, but he just left the comment hanging. 'So, as I said on the phone. Thanks for getting in touch. I had been meaning to try myself, but time just kind of got away from me. Do you get recognised a lot, by the way?'

'What do you mean?' Johnny asked.

'Daphne, she recognised you, from Swerve, I mean.'

'Really, do you think so?'

'I know so. When my mate tipped me off that you were looking for me, I realised I already knew who you were because of Swerve. I know you weren't huge, but you were on TV a few times, and definitely in the *NME*. What I hadn't realised was that you were my son, because I thought he was called Johnny Brown. Anyway, people would recognise you, particularly younger people, but maybe not be able to put a name to the face.'

Johnny recognised a hint of pride in Marty's voice.

'Well done anyway.'

'Well done for what?'

'For making it in the business. I've been trying for decades but never quite got there.'

Johnny looked at Marty smiling at him and felt a surge of emotion; tears were rapidly rising to the surface. He was not generally a crier, so this genuinely took him aback. He tried to swallow them away, but he could feel them hovering. Marty seemed oblivious.

'You know, when I met your mother, I was convinced I was going to make it. It was the mid-sixties, and there was music everywhere. I was in several bands around Hastings and Brighton, but none of them ever quite hit the big time. I'm still playing now, still hoping. I envy you, you've already done it, so whatever happens you can look back on those years at the top with Swerve and know that you did it.'

'Thanks, Marty, kind words. I'd never really seen it from that perspective. I'm still a bit bitter and twisted about the Swerve split. To be honest, I'd like to get back to where I was before the bust-up. You know I played last night at –'

Marty interrupted, 'Enjoy it while you can. It all gets harder as you get older. I still just about make a living doing some gigs and selling a few paintings, but it's not easy.'

Johnny had been on the cusp of telling Marty how well he thought the gig had gone last night, but it seemed like the wrong moment. The slight change in mood had at least pushed his own emotions back under the surface. The food arrived, so they started to tuck in. Johnny watched Marty as he ate and told him about his musical career, a tale of near misses, fallings-out and opportunities squandered. He was a good storyteller, quite charming, if a little egocentric. It was obvious to Johnny that he was hearing one side of each tale only. However, he could see how Mary might have fallen for a younger Marty, a perhaps more upbeat Marty, a young man convinced that he had a life of fame and fortune in front of him. Johnny was not sure if he should start to quiz him about meeting his mother and the time they spent together before Johnny was born. He needn't have worried.

'It was the lure of the bright lights that took me away from your mother back then. I was asked to go on a tour in the US with a band called Wild Storm. Their guitarist had taken one acid trip too many and needed some time getting his head back together. They were from London, and everyone in the scene thought they were one step from hitting it big. A tour in the US would be the thing that made it happen. So I talked to your mother about it, and she agreed I should do this one tour with them for a couple of months then come back before you were born. Well, what can I say? It never turned out like that, as you know. Somehow a couple of months turned into a couple of years. We didn't even have a phone at our flat in Hastings, so I wrote Mary letters to keep in touch, but I was moving around a lot, and things just petered out. In the end, so much time had passed I think I was just too embarrassed to get back in touch when I knew I was coming back to the UK. I wasn't very good at thinking about other people when I was that age. Some might say I'm still not very good at it.'

Johnny was really trying not to be judgemental, to give Marty some space to tell his own story, but all he could think of was how his mother must have struggled as a single parent. He knew his gran and grandad had helped enormously, but he imagined how lonely his mother must have been on her own. She was used to it now, but then she would have been in her early twenties. A child herself still, on her own with a baby.

'Didn't you even try to get back in touch?' Johnny couldn't help asking.

'It's a long time ago now, but I do remember calling a couple of times when I got back to Blighty, but Mary was having none of it. Gave me short shrift. So I just moved on . . .' Marty tailed off. He pushed his empty plate away and lit another cigarette. He was still an attractive man, well dressed in a bohemian way, with a silk scarf tied at his neck, a denim shirt, brown suede jacket and tight Levi's. He was lean and chiselled, but his face was starting to show his age, his brown eyes crinkled at the edges, his sculpted cheeks etched a little with broken veins and his shoulder-length brown hair thinning slightly. Johnny imagined he had been a handsome devil in his prime.

'What are you doing at the moment?' Johnny decided to get things back to the present and give Marty a bit of a break.

'Well, I'm living on my own, just down the road in a nice council flat. Not one of the modern ones. It's a Victorian conversion. I'm lucky to have it. I could buy it off the council and make a fast buck, but I'm not really interested. I'd rather not have the hassle. I'm in a couple of bands with regular gigs – you know, covers for functions, that kind of thing – and I'm still selling a bit of art, abstract oils. There's a handful of galleries around town that take them. Life treats me pretty well really. I never quite made it, but there's lots of people worse off than me.'

'It sounds like you have a pretty decent thing going. You're doing the things you like doing anyway. That must be good.'

'That's exactly what I think, but I haven't found a lady yet who shares that opinion.'

'You're not married then? Or living with anyone?'

'Well, I never married your mother. We weren't together long enough really, and no, no one since. There have been women over the years, a couple of whom I was really in love with for a while, but they never seem to last. My lack of aspiration seems to be a common theme. I'm also a bit of a sucker for a pretty girl with a nice smile. That's caught me out a few times, too.'

His mother's hints over the years about his father's character were finally being confirmed first hand. At least he was open and honest, if not terribly fatherly. Johnny was not sure what to make of it all. He decided to keep it less personal. 'So are you into contemporary art?'

'I'm into any kind of art.'

'The reason I ask is because I've got to know some of the YBAs.'

'Ah, yes, the Young British Artists, fakers or fortune-makers. Who do you know?'

'Well, I know several on nodding terms, but Arthur Swale, the sculptor, is a proper friend.'

'Ah yes, *The Narcissist*. I liked it when I saw it at the Royal Academy. Beautifully made.'

'You went to the *Sensation* exhibition?'

'Oh yes, I love a big exhibition like that. The Hirsts I really liked, the Myra Hindley, too. Not so sure about Tracey Emin or Sarah Lucas. There was lots of other interesting stuff, though. Chris Ofili, Marc Quinn, you know, the head made out of frozen blood. I really enjoyed the whole exhibition.'

'I went with Sophie and a couple of friends. Arthur invited us to the opening.'

'Sophie's your wife?'

Johnny realised suddenly that Marty knew nothing about him.

'Yes, sorry, I'm married to Sophie, and we have a daughter, Amy.'

'So, I'm a grandad? I'll keep that quiet, else it will cramp my style.'

Marty laughed, and Johnny tried to laugh along. In reality he was upset that Marty wasn't more interested in his granddaughter. He changed the subject back to art again.

'Sophie's going to Arthur Swale's exhibition in Paris in a few days. A couple of friends of mine have organised it.'

'Sounds like you're a bit of a jetsetter to me. You said Sophie's going. Aren't you going, too?'

'Well, I wasn't going to.'

'Why the hell not? Don't give up a chance like that. A few days in Paris in the spring. What could be better?'

Before he knew it the words were out of his mouth. 'Why don't we both go? You could come with us?'

***

Sophie was still in a state of shock. The last few days had been a whirlwind of meeting Marty, organising Marty's, Johnny's and her own travel arrangements, getting Amy to her mother's for a couple of nights, speaking to Juste, Mark and Henri about arrangements for Arthur's opening night and now, finally, they were on the Eurostar, in first class no less, sipping on glasses of champagne as their train hurtled towards the tunnel at Folkstone. They had boarded the train at Ashford International after Marty had overnighted with them in Brede, meeting her and Amy for the first time. She looked at him as he and Johnny chatted animatedly across the table between them. There was something about Marty that she instinctively distrusted. She wasn't sure if it was founded on his history as an absent father or drawn from her recent acquaintance with the man himself, but he seemed slippery. He was quite vague, particularly when it came to the past, where he had lived, what he had got up to, who his significant others were. None of these questions elicited direct responses. It made Sophie uncomfortable, as Johnny himself was going out on a limb for Marty. It was typical of Johnny; he never did things by half. It had seriously upset his mother when Johnny had told her that he had reconnected with Marty; even more so when he had then told Mary that they were taking Marty to Paris for the opening of an art exhibition. Communications between them had been temporarily suspended. She was still speaking to Sophie and still helping with Amy when needed, but Johnny was getting the silent treatment. Sophie looked at Marty as he spoke; she watched as he closed his eyes while still speaking, and he only briefly maintained eye contact with Johnny even when his eyes were open. He had been charming to her as soon as they had met, and she could see what Mary had fallen for as a young woman. His full physical glory had now faded, but his bone structure, slim build and bohemian look were still on show. She was surprised that his genetic influence on Johnny extended beyond just looks; there were other similarities. They had the same smile, which came easily to both of them, the same gesticulations when talking, almost Mediterranean rather than northern European in their extravagant hand movements. It gave both of them an artistic, creative look. Johnny's fair colouring reminded her of his mother, and his eyes were blue while Marty's were brown, but there was a look that they shared. There was no doubting that they were father and son. She would keep an eye on Marty. Johnny was generous with his emotions, and she did not want his generosity exploited.

Her thoughts turned to the evening's events. She would be seeing Juste in person for the first time since last autumn when they had kissed. She had thought a lot about that moment since then. They had spoken on the phone in the meantime, but Juste had just carried on as normal with no reference to what had happened. Juste admitting that night to 'straying' on a regular basis made Sophie feel that for Juste it was probably just a passing flirtation that had come to nothing. For Sophie it had been more meaningful, something she found hard to forget, both physically and emotionally. She was nervous about seeing Juste, but the thought of being in Paris without seeing her was impossible. Henri, on the other hand, she felt surprisingly indifferent towards. She had convinced herself that she had probably never been in love with Henri, and that he had definitely never been in love with her. When she was recovering from the hurt of seeing Johnny and Mark together, and when Johnny himself had been completely off the rails at the end of the Swerve era, she had looked to Henri as a shoulder to cry on. While he had not been a great listener, he had made her feel wanted, desired and appreciated. Even if it had been largely physical, the desire he felt for her had given her confidence when she had been at a low ebb. But why had they continued their affair after she had got back together with Johnny? For her part she thought it was for the thrill, the excitement of the covert meetings. She had also found him desirable, his arrogance attractive, his accent seductive; he had been her window into a fantasy world of smart hotels, gastronomic dinners and fine wine. His renewed friendship with Mark had put her off for sure, but that was not the only thing. There was something about Henri that lacked authenticity; he was always trying to win. Not just when they had played poker together with the others but also in life, in relationships, he wanted to have the upper hand. She hadn't cared at first, but as she regained her own confidence it had started to irk her. Johnny was the opposite. He wasn't trying to win anything; he was just trying to have the best time he could and hoped that the people around him shared in that. He bore no long-term grudges; he forgave easily. Juste, she realised, was more like Johnny. She wasn't trying to own Sophie, she was simply attracted to her and acting on instinct. Some people were simpler in a way, untethered, freed from the humdrum emotions such as guilt, jealousy and remorse. She wished she could be more like them, but she knew she wasn't. Her Catholic upbringing did not help when it came to guilt – the French side of her family were responsible for that. She was excited at seeing Juste but felt guilty about Véronique. If Juste were to be believed, she didn't need to, but she did and would.

She tuned back into Johnny's conversation with Marty. He was still calling him Marty rather than Dad, she noticed, which she thought was a good thing. As they hurtled towards Paris at 300 km/h Sophie felt the anticipation of the event filling her with a mixture of nerves and excitement. Whatever happened with Juste, she would soon be back in Paris, with people she loved, despite their flaws.

***

Mark realised that for a gay man (and he really felt now that he was a gay man, not a bisexual man, a gay man attracted to other men and not to women) he was not great at a lot of the things that gay men were stereotypically known for. He really could not rely on his own dress sense. As a result, he had adopted what he knew was quite a boring approach to clothes, but in doing so he had more or less eliminated the risk of looking foolish. He rarely strayed from the colour palette blue, and he rarely deviated from two types of outfits: suits for work – dark with white shirts and blue ties – and jeans and a button-down shirt for casual, sometimes a sweater over the shirt then a casual zip-up leather jacket. He had realised and also been told (mainly by Johnny) not to go for the complicated traps he had fallen into with leather jackets, like stone-wash, epaulettes, multiple zips, padded shoulders; once he reached his thirties the penny had dropped, and he now went for a straightforward zip-up leather jackets without any baubles. He looked in the mirror in the hotel room. Shoes had continued to be a problem until he discovered brogues. He now wore black brogues for work and brown brogues for casual. Tonight, because it was a casual outfit, he was wearing a black shirt, black leather jacket, jeans and brown brogues. He hoped Arthur liked how he looked, although he couldn't remember Arthur ever commenting on how he was dressed. Arthur had already gone to the venue, so he couldn't check. Arthur had been wearing his own uniform of battered parka, jeans and steel toe cap boots. He would just go with it. They weren't a sartorial couple, and it didn't seem to bother either of them. He had started wearing his hair a bit longer since he and Arthur had got together, but he suspected he still had the air of an off-duty accountant. Arthur just looked a bit scruffy and slightly crazed. Henri would no doubt look his normal elegant self at the exhibition, while Johnny would certainly look the epitome of cool. Sophie would be in vintage, carrying it off with her usual panache. Some people just had style, and he was happy to admit that he was not one of them. As he stood contemplating himself in the hotel room mirror, he thought it was strange that he had ended up with such stylish friends.

He had checked the map in his guidebook, and from their hotel at Place des Vosges, the Pavillon de la Reine, the Galerie Schmidt was only a ten-minute walk. Mark was slightly overwhelmed by the luxury of the hotel, but Henri had insisted on putting them up there. He always seemed to know someone who knew someone who could get you into these places at a good rate – or maybe it was a contact of Caroline's – in any case it was probably the smartest hotel he had ever stayed in. The gallery was close to the Pompidou Centre, which Arthur had pointed out to him from the taxi on the way to the hotel. The Centre had reminded him of the Lloyd's Building in the City, and Arthur had explained that the reason for that was because they were designed by the same British architect, Richard Rogers. It would be hard for him to get lost as this building was such a prominent landmark. He left the hotel early as he wanted to be there to support Arthur in the nervous period before everyone arrived. Not that Arthur seemed to get nervous. This was the biggest solo exhibition Arthur had ever held, as far as he knew, but he treated it as if it were the same as any other. Mark could tell that he was excited, but he didn't really discuss his feelings with him. His excitement was betrayed by an increase in the level of his manic side. He became even more obsessive than normal about his art. Mark had not seen the exhibits, other than *The Narcissist*, which he had only ever seen at the *Sensation* exhibition. Arthur had discussed the generality of what he was doing, they hadn't discussed the specifics. While Mark understood why he would do this, he did feel a little excluded. He knew that Henri and Caroline had been to the studio and seen the works, and when he had spoken to Henri about this Henri had seemed very upbeat, but he had made it clear that he was under strict instructions not to discuss details with anyone. Mark walked quickly down Rue des Francs-Bourgeois, the busy, narrow street bustling around him in the early-spring-evening light. He felt like he might burst with expectation.

***

Henri helped himself to a glass of champagne as the servers began to pour them in advance of the guests arriving. Caroline was busy checking with her staff on the last-minute arrangements. He watched as she moved with her purposeful gait, as tall as most of the men in the room in her heels. She definitely had a presence; she wore a little black dress, classically French in style, with the skirt quite short to accentuate her long legs, which shimmered in sheer black stockings. Henri was waiting for the right moment to invite her to dinner *à deux*. He hoped that a successful exhibition tonight would increase the chances of that happening. He also had another tactic up his sleeve. He had invited Emily, his occasional girlfriend, to the opening, and she had gladly accepted. He would see how Caroline reacted to another woman in his company. The presence of Emily would also help, he hoped, to show Sophie that he knew it was over between them and that it was no big deal.

He turned to the end of the large room where the exhibits were currently hidden behind a semi-circular curtain. There had been a certain amount of cloak and dagger about exactly how things were to be positioned. Arthur had insisted that he should have the last say on this and also that the final arrangements should be made by him, assisted only by one of Caroline's staff. Henri was amused by this; he knew Arthur well enough by now to realise that there was a surprise in store, but he had no idea what it might be. He lit a Disque Bleu with a smile. Out of the corner of his eye he saw Mark arrive and went over to greet him, picking up another glass of champagne on the way.

'Good evening, Monsieur Arnold.' He kissed Mark on both cheeks, as was his habit with his closer male friends. Mark was always a little flustered by this.

'Hi, Henri. I don't think I'm ever going to get used to your Gallic welcome.'

'That's what makes you the man you are, Mark.' Henri laughed and handed him the champagne.

'How is your hotel?'

'It's wonderful. Way too good for us.'

'Well, Arthur is the man of the moment. He deserves it.'

'Are Johnny and Sophie staying there, too? I haven't spoken to Johnny.'

'Yes, and there is a surprise guest.'

'Really? Who's that?'

'It's Johnny's dad!'

'Wow, really? I knew he was meeting up with him. You know he never met him until a week ago?'

'It seems they are now best buddies. And how is your *amour*, Arthur? Nervous, excited, neither?'

'Well, he's been quite secretive, to be honest. I haven't even seen the art. You're one of the lucky few.'

'Apparently so. I haven't seen him. He must be preparing for the big reveal.'

From nowhere Emily appeared, looking cute and pleased to see him. She was such a nice girl, way too nice for him. He kissed her warmly on the lips and inhaled the aroma of her blonde hair. He smelled the familiar smell that always reminded him of Provence. He introduced Emily to Mark. 'Mark, this is Emily Witter, an old friend from Geneva.'

Emily shook hands with Mark. Her English was excellent, just a slight, almost imperceptible accent, not French, much harder to place. She was accomplished as well as pretty. Why was it that Henri wasn't more drawn to her? He felt a tap on his shoulder, and there were Johnny, Sophie and, he presumed, Johnny's father. The gang was all here.

'My two best friends standing together, what could be better.' Johnny gave Henri and Mark an effusive welcome, hugging each in turn. Then he turned proudly to his dad. 'And this is Marty, my new dad. Well, my old dad, but new to me, if you know what I mean.'

'I think they know what you mean,' said Marty softly, shaking hands with Mark, Henri and Emily, in turn.

Sophie quietly greeted them, too, kissing all three of them on each cheek. She gave Henri a knowing smile. So, they were still friends at least.

'So where have you been hiding Emily, Henri?'

'She lives in Geneva, if that is what you mean?'

Johnny was in one of his larger-than-life moods, it seemed; these were normally fuelled by booze and/or coke. Henri could see Emily cringing a little as she smiled. He led everyone over to get drinks to ease Emily's pain. He hoped Johnny would not embarrass him in front of Caroline and her Paris art crowd. The great and the good of the city were now arriving, and the room was filling up. Showtime was upon them.

***

Sophie suddenly felt an arm around her waist. She recognised the touch immediately and felt her senses heighten. It was Juste.

'You look ravishing, my darling,' she whispered in her ear. Juste had adopted the look that had first attracted Sophie to her in the bar at Le Meurice a few years ago. She had dyed her hair black, and it was slicked back; she wore a dinner suit, a dress shirt and a bootlace tie. She looked sexy and powerful.

'You do, too,' Sophie whispered back before greeting Véronique.

'Is that the cheating husband?' Juste nodded towards Johnny.

'Yes, it is.'

'Well, I'm glad it's not the other guy next to him.'

'No, that's Mark.'

'The queer?'

'Yes.'

'He's very badly dressed for a queer guy.'

'Yes, I know. That's just the way Mark is. He's an accountant.'

'He certainly dresses like one.'

Juste hugged Sophie and kissed her on each cheek.

'Johnny!' she called her husband over. He walked towards them smiling. Mark remained hovering next to Marty.

'May I introduce you to Juste and Véronique. You've already had their rave reviews from me, now you finally get to meet them.' Sophie spoke in English for Johnny's sake, although he did speak rudimentary French.

'I've heard so much about you two, but I had never realised how beautiful you both were. *Vraiment très belles.*' Johnny could turn on the charm when necessary. The two women beamed as Johnny kissed them. Sophie realised how much easier it was for men to compliment French women on their appearance. She doubted that Johnny would have said the same to two English women of the same age; they might have thought it was a little cheesy.

'Well, it's not every day we meet a real pop star, so delighted to meet you, too.' Juste was also on a charm offensive.

'I shouldn't leave Marty on his own at the moment,' Johnny said to Sophie. 'Great to meet you two finally. See you later on. Enjoy the unveiling!'

Sophie reverted to French. 'He's just met his dad for the first time ever, so he insisted on bringing him here. It's all still very new.'

Juste raised one eyebrow. 'Your husband is quite complicated. Handsome, cool but quite complicated.'

Sophie laughed. It was a pretty accurate description of Johnny. Despite everything, she loved him for it.

'Les BCBG sont là en masse. Il y a moins des Bobos.'

Véronique was scanning the crowd. Sophie knew the BCBG acronym in French translated broadly to Sloane Rangers in the UK, and there were a number of people who fitted that description just by their appearance. Men in handmade shoes and tailored suits, and women wearing heirloom jewellery and Chanel two-piece outfits. Bobo Sophie was not familiar with.

'What's a Bobo?' she asked.

It was Juste who answered. 'Bourgeois bohemians. People like you, Sophie.'

Véronique laughed loudly.

'I think we both might fit that description,' Sophie said to Juste. Véronique laughed even louder.

The lights in the room started to dim, and the hubbub in the room quietened. The first bars of 'It's a Sin' by the Pet Shop Boys started to reverberate around the room.

***

As the music started Mark felt the nerves in the pit of his stomach. He had no idea what was going to happen next. He listened to the opening keyboard chords, and, on the cue of the small explosion in the introduction of the song, the curtains started to move slowly. Lights flashed then a spotlight began to focus in on the gap in the curtains, gradually illuminating *The Narcissist*, its metal frame shining in the light, with the yellow-coloured water from the metal penis glistening as it flowed into the sculpture's mouth. It was really quite dramatic, but Mark thought he could make out a shadow just in front and a little to the side. He was proved right as a second spotlight suddenly brought the object of the shadow into view. It was a naked man mimicking the position of the sculpture, his shoulders and head to the floor supporting the remainder of his body with his hands placed on his back as his buttocks and legs reached upwards. Mark knew immediately that he had seen this man naked before, it was Arthur.

As the spotlight highlighted him with more definition, a gasp went up from the assembled crowd, who were only a matter of yards away after all. Mark could see a liquid spurting from the area of Arthur's genitals towards his open mouth; surely he wasn't pissing into his own mouth? He quickly noticed that there was something attached to Arthur's penis. It looked like a flower. The liquid was coming from a joke plastic buttonhole flower attached to the end of Arthur's dick. Mark was not sure how, but somehow Arthur was manipulating the squeezy bulb at the other end of the joke flower apparatus to produce the effect that he was, indeed, pissing into his own mouth. The liquid certainly had a yellowy tinge to it. More lights were now coming on to spotlight a series of other works that quickly appeared one after another placed in a semi-circle behind *The Narcissist*. Mark counted seven in all: so these were the seven deadly sins. The crowd of invitees responded noisily to all this with cheers and whistles as the whole display was revealed. Surely this was unusually rowdy for an art-gallery crowd. It was hard for Mark to take it all in as the lights gradually came up. He felt quite emotional. The Pet Shop Boys faded out to be followed by the opening bars of what he recognised as 'Jump Around' by House of Pain. As the chorus came on Arthur bounced up from his narcissistic position and literally began to jump around, his flowered penis bouncing as he did so. This was obviously enough for Caroline Schmidt who arrived as if from nowhere with a bathrobe, which she helped Arthur into. She then raised Arthur's hand above his head, like a boxer in triumph, to a huge round of applause accompanied by more whistles and cheers. This could not have gone any better, thought Mark. Arthur was being feted like some kind of hero of the art world. He went over to congratulate him, but it looked as if he would have to join the queue.

***

Henri could see from the look on Caroline's face that the opening had exceeded her expectations. His heart had been in his mouth as the second spotlight homed in on Arthur's naked body; it had not returned to his chest until Caroline had entered the scene with the bathrobe. Now he was elated. He had been kept in the dark about exactly what would happen at the opening, but clearly Caroline had been in the know. She had moved away from Arthur now and was beaming as she was approached and congratulated by guests as they moved in to get a better look at the exhibits. He would leave it a while before he went over to congratulate her, too. He could tell that she was loving the reflected glory created by a successful opening. It was unusual for a Paris art crowd to be so noisy; somehow Arthur had struck a chord with these rather snooty Parisians and had managed to pull off a bit of a coup. This could only be good for Henri, good financially and good in his pursuit of Caroline. She would be pumped tonight by the adrenaline coursing through her, and he would make sure that he was close by her for the rest of the evening, reminding her who had been responsible for her success.

***

'You absolute fucker.' Johnny grabbed Arthur in a big bear hug.

'It seemed to go down quite well.' Arthur was chuckling away. He was still stood in front of *The Narcissist* in his bathrobe. Behind him people were milling around the other works gesticulating enthusiastically.

'It just shows the power of acting like a fuckin' idiot.'

Marty appeared next to Johnny.

‘This is Marty, my dad.’ The two artists nodded at one another. Johnny had the impression that they were sizing one another up.

‘Powerful stuff, Arthur. Well done. It reminds me of some of the things we were doing in the early seventies.’ Marty clearly wanted it known that he wasn’t just an art lover but an actual artist.

‘Is that right?’ said Arthur. ‘Were you using joke flowers on your cocks then, too.’ Arthur took no prisoners. Johnny winced a little. He watched as Marty smiled thinly.

‘Anyway, I’m off to put some clothes on. I’ll catch up again when I’m fully dressed.’

With that Arthur was gone.

‘Let’s have a good look at the rest of the stuff then, shall we, Marty,’ Johnny said as they moved towards the other works. Johnny was immediately struck by the power of what Arthur had created as he began to walk among the seven new sculptures. He stood next to a model of what looked to Johnny like a figure in some kind of ceremonial military dress, possibly a high-ranking First World War officer, with knee-length leather boots, green breeches that ballooned out from the knee and a military jacket covered in medals, ribbon, gold-braided cord and shiny, bright gold buttons. Johnny imagined a general forcing his troops out of the trenches over the top into no man’s land. The head of the general supported an elaborate cap with more military decoration above a crazed-looking, ruddy-cheeked face, festooned with a handlebar moustache. It looked as if the model had been made with papier mâché. The figure was saluting into a full-length mirror, and a second mirror had been placed behind in such a way as to create an infinite number of images of the saluting general reflecting back and forth. With his head at the correct angle Johnny could see hundreds of images of the general as they marched into infinity. Burnt into the back of his green military jacket was the word PRIDE. Johnny was genuinely moved by the overall effect; the ridiculous, proud general made him feel how ludicrous the whole military establishment was, its enforced discipline based on the pride of the men at the top.

He looked at Marty next to him, who was peering quizzically at the piece. He took a pair of half-moon glasses from his jacket pocket, homing in on the detailing.

'What do you think?' Johnny asked him.

'I think the image is powerful, but I'm not sure about the quality of the finish. It looks a bit amateurish.'

'Don't you think the finish is part of the impression the artist wants to give, almost a bit amusement arcade, a bit hall of mirrors?'

'Well, I just think it could have had a better finish.'

Johnny got the impression that Marty hadn't really listened to what he had said and wasn't prepared to take on a different view to his own. In the short time they had known one another he had realised that Marty was not the world's greatest listener. They moved on to the next exhibit. It was a life-size mechanical figure constructed from Arthur's trademark Meccano-like metalwork. On each side of the figure was a small pile of what looked like gold bars. The figure lifted all the gold bars from the pile on one side to create a pile on the other side, paused, then lifted all the bars back to make a pile back on the other side. There were twenty or so bars, and the whole process lasted only a few minutes. As he watched Johnny realised that each bar had the word GREED stamped into it. Although the figure was very simply made, it must have taken some engineering ingenuity to design it to make the movements necessary to complete the stacking and unstacking of the bars. Arthur really was a clever guy, despite all his northern bluff.

'How about this one, Marty?' Johnny said, after they had watched the figure follow its monotonous task a couple of times. He had found the process calming and almost hypnotic, although the underlying message of the relentless quest for material wealth had not passed him by. However, he wanted to hear Marty's initial thoughts before he commented on the piece himself.

'The message is a little simplistic,' Marty said. 'Gold bars equals greed. It's not that far-reaching a thought, is it?'

'I was thinking that the simplicity highlights the message. People lead repetitious lives, all in the name of stacking up the cash. Capitalism is relentless, a relentless pursuit of more and more cash, or, in this case, gold bars. I like it. I think it captures the ethos of our modern world. I also find it strangely calming to watch.'

'Well, that's another way of looking at it, I suppose.' Marty moved on to the next exhibit. Johnny had realised that Marty did not particularly enjoy an opinion that differed from his own. He wondered if that was the result of living by himself and not having his views questioned very often, a kind of habit he had got into. Or maybe it was an indication of a more deep-seated egocentric character. He might ask his mum about that once they were talking again. He could tell that Sophie was not all that enthusiastic about Marty, but he would persevere. Everyone had their unappealing traits as well as those that were more attractive.

***

Mark finally had the chance to catch up with Arthur as he came out of the makeshift dressing-room that normally functioned as a broom cupboard. He had spotted Arthur slip in there and was waiting outside for him. As Arthur emerged, now fully clothed, he gave him a big bear hug. He knew Arthur didn't like public displays of affection between them, but he couldn't help himself. For once Arthur did not try to wrestle out of his grasp but hugged him back. Mark could feel Arthur's emotion through his body. He released him and looked into his eyes.

'That was fucking amazing. Well done, mate. The crowd loved it.'

To Mark's surprise Arthur looked to be tearing up at little, clearly overwhelmed.

'I need to get a fuckin' grip. I don't want these French cunts thinkin' I've gone soft.'

Mark laughed as Arthur rubbed his eyes and slapped himself about the face a couple of times.

'It has gone down well, though, it seems. Caroline told me she has interest in some pieces already. It's such a relief. I've been working on this for years without knowing if the idea was going to fly. I mean, I think the pieces are fuckin' great, but it nice to know that some other people think the same. Preferably a few with fat wallets.'

After briefly showing a glimpse of vulnerability, Arthur was now reverting to type.

Mark smiled at him. 'I think the whole thing has been stunning, from your naked narcissist right through each of the seven deadly sins. It's been a revelation. I was a bit pissed off that you had kept it all so secret from me, but it was worth it. It's been thrilling, really thrilling. What a night.'

'What's the plan for later? I could do with a few fuckin' drinks, mate, I don't know about you.'

'I think Henri has organised something for later after the guests have left. That must be quite soon. I can see that people are starting to drift off. Why don't you go and take a bit more praise before they've all gone. Come on, I can see Henri and Caroline talking to some potential buyers. Let's see what gives.'

***

Henri knew that it was a little rude to neglect Emily, but nevertheless he had left her with Sophie, Juste and Véronique. He would make up for lost time later. He knew that his timing with Caroline was at a crucial point. His star was in the ascendant, and he wanted to make sure that Caroline recognised that he had played an important part in the great success of the evening. He had just introduced her to one of his banking customers, Édouard Fontaine, who had a keen interest in contemporary art, as much for its speculative-investment potential as for its artistic content.

Édouard was riding the new wave of hedge funds that were hitting the international market, which meant he had deep pockets. A Parisian by birth, he had recently moved to London, where he had bought an enormous warehouse apartment in Wapping overlooking the River Thames. This meant he had plenty of space to fill with art. He was a perfect match for Caroline, as they would know many of the same people. Henri had learned over the last few years that name dropping was the social convention in this world. People that you had been introduced to once were described as friends; if you had had lunch with someone they became a great friend. He listened as Caroline and Édouard verbally exchanged the contacts in their Filofaxes in an escalating war of one-upmanship. Right on cue Arthur arrived with Mark tailing him.

'How goes it, Henri? Hope you enjoyed that.' Henri couldn't have been more delighted at the clear demonstration to Édouard that he and the artist really were great friends. He immediately introduced Arthur and Mark to Édouard; he described Mark as Arthur's business manager, which was loosely correct.

'I loved the show, especially your participation.' Édouard spoke in lightly accented English. 'I was saying to Caroline, I'm interested in investing, but I like to think big. Do you have more work in the pipeline?'

'To be honest, mate, I've been flat out on this for a while. But I've got lots of ideas. If I had some cash and more help, there's loads of things I'd love to build.'

'Well, I love the authenticity of your work, the honesty of it. I understand that Mr Saatchi owns *The Narcissist*, but the rest is for sale?'

'As far as I know. My team deals with the sales. I don't get involved. You would have to discuss that with Caroline. I'm just the fuckin' artist, mate.' Arthur laughed his big laugh, and they all joined him, Mark, Henri, Édouard and even Caroline.

Édouard began to speak French directly to Caroline. 'I am

seriously interested in buying all seven *Deadly Sins*. Let's discuss this tomorrow. Please don't sell any of them until we have spoken.'

'Of course, Édouard.'

Henri saw Mark looking at him quizzically. His French obviously wasn't good enough to keep up with the conversation. He winked at him and grinned. Mark grinned back. Caroline and Édouard were still deep in conversation. Henri put his hands lightly on one shoulder each of Mark and Arthur and ushered them away to a distance.

'Edouard wants to buy them all,' he said quietly as soon as they were out of earshot. 'We already have buyers for some of the pieces individually, so we'll probably go to sealed bids. The highest bidder wins. I think they'll go for double or treble the price that we were asking.'

'Wow!' Mark was clearly astonished.

'But do you think this guy Édouard really likes them?' asked Arthur.

'Who gives a fuck. We're going to make lots of money, Arthur.' As soon as he said it Henri realised that he had screwed up. He had meant what he said in a jokey kind of way, but Arthur had taken it to heart. Arthur was a purist, a real artist, Henri should have known not to joke about the art. He was also volatile.

'I give a fuck. You fuckin' money men are all the same,' Arthur reacted straight away. He turned on his heel and walked off.

Mark followed in his wake. 'Well done, Henri,' Mark called over his shoulder as he chased after his furious lover.

Henri hoped Caroline had not noticed their spat and saw to his relief that she was still deep in conversation with Édouard. He walked back over. Édouard was a serial adulterer, and, despite the fact that he was in early fifties, he would see Caroline as fair game. Henri did not need any more problems to solve this evening. He would smooth it over with Arthur; he wasn't such a purist that he had an aversion to being paid. Maybe the angle to take was to emphasise how much funding it would give him for the next collection. He would find a way. He would also invite Caroline to the Buddha-Bar later, but not Édouard.

***

Sophie was enjoying the buzz of their return to the Buddha-Bar. As evening turned to night the volume of the music rose, and the crowd gradually became more unruly. Underworld's 'Born Slippy' was playing, one of the few tracks she had immediately recognised that night, although she was loving the music. She let the hypnotic beat of the song seep through her. Juste had offered her some ecstasy earlier, but she felt like she had no need for it; she was high on a few glasses of champagne and the thrill of being in Paris. She surveyed their table. There seemed to have been words exchanged between Henri, Mark and Arthur earlier, but they were now chatting and laughing amiably enough. She would try to find out from Johnny later what had been going on. Caroline, to Sophie's surprise, had actually joined them, albeit belatedly. She could tell from Henri's body language that he was in pursuit of her, but there were no signs yet that he had managed to reel her in. Sophie had found the brief exchanges she had had with Caroline quite frosty and suspected that her warmth was reserved for people with a bigger art budget than her own. Or maybe she knew that something had happened between her and Henri. To her right Johnny and Marty were still deep in conversation, latterly, from what she could hear, about guitars. To her left sat Juste, whose body was pushed up tightly against hers, while opposite them were Véronique and Emily, an unlikely pairing, who seemed to be getting on like a house on fire. It was hard not to love Véronique, even if, like Emily, you had grown up in Geneva's slightly austere culture. Just as she was smiling to herself at how cute they looked, they jumped up in unison and exclaimed that they were going to dance.

'Fucking flirt. Look at her,' Juste said into Sophie's ear. 'Follow me.' She took Sophie firmly by the hand and walked with her over to the ladies. As soon as they were inside Juste walked into a cubicle, still holding Sophie's hand, locked the door and gently pushed her against the partition. Sophie did nothing to resist as Juste kissed her on the mouth, at first gently then harder. Sophie felt herself responding, immediately aroused by this sudden assault. She kissed Juste back, hard, too, and felt Juste react by pushing her body into Sophie's.

Juste, broke away suddenly and exclaimed loudly, '*Quelle sale pute!*' which Sophie loosely translated as 'What a fucking slut' before going back to kissing her with increasing passion. Sophie quickly realised it was Véronique not her she was calling a slut; she wasn't talking dirty.

The adolescent-style clinch carried on for some time before they broke off, panting a little, their clothing in some disarray, before Sophie eventually said, 'I think we ought to go back inside, don't you?'

'I guess so,' said Juste, touching Sophie's face affectionately before kissing her one last time. She pushed Sophie's fringe gently away from her eyes, looked deep into her eyes and slowly began to do up the buttons she had undone. Sophie did the same for Juste. Then, finally, they pushed the creases out of one another's clothes, laughed and unlocked the cubicle door. As they left the loo and walked back into the club, they could see that Véronique and Emily were still on the dancefloor, clearly oblivious to what might be happening elsewhere.

'*Sale pute!*' Juste shouted at the top of her voice to no one in particular but was drowned out by the music. She grabbed Sophie's hand again and walked possessively back to their table. The others were all still absorbed in the same conversations they had been in when they had left. They sat back down, and Juste immediately put her arm around Sophie. It could have been friendly, but Sophie could tell that it was more than that. She wondered what she was doing; she definitely had a crush on Juste, but should she be responding to her like this? There were others to think of – Véronique for one, but Johnny, too, and, of course, Amy. She needed to be careful not to get carried away in the moment. But Juste was so charismatic, her big personality acted like a magnet, and it had drawn Sophie in. In a way she felt a closer connection than she might have done with a man; there was an understanding between two women that was somehow more intimate. Perhaps she was just a little lonely. Johnny could be distant from their relationship, particularly when he was working on his music. Her feelings for Juste were confusing, but she was drawn to her all the same.

***

Henri had never seen Caroline so relaxed; she was even a little drunk. It enhanced her appeal to him, seeing her loosen up a little, still very elegant and controlled but softer and less buttoned-up. He watched as she reacted to Arthur's latest anecdote about growing up in Scunthorpe.

'Then I just fuckin' chinned him,' Arthur was saying. It sounded like a punchline. Mark was laughing.

'But what does chinned mean?' Caroline asked, not following him.

'I fuckin' punched him in the face.' As he said it Arthur pretended to give Mark a right-hander, stopping a couple of inches away from his face. Caroline thought this was hilarious, although Mark looked a little taken aback. Henri smiled, he had been deep in thought until the punchline and so had no idea whether or not the story had been as funny as Caroline thought. He watched her as she laughed; she really was getting under his skin.

Later, back at his apartment, Henri lay on his back looking at the ceiling. Emily was next to him in bed breathing softly. They had kissed a little before she slept, but she had said she was tired, and Henri's heart was not in it either. Maybe their time was nearly up, thought Henri, but it had been good that she had been there with him. Caroline had definitely noticed. He had asked her for dinner the following night as they left the Buddha-Bar, ostensibly to discuss the aftermath of the exhibition, but the fact that he had asked her to dinner meant there was an imperceptible shift in the dynamic of their relationship. Dinner was not lunch. Lunch was a business appointment; dinner was subtly different. He would be patient, but he would have her.

***

Sophie took the bottle of white wine from the fridge. It was a Sancerre, an immediate reminder of France and, more to the point, the trip to Paris. It had been a long way home with a hangover, particularly the train to London, where Sophie thought even Johnny's tolerance of Marty had started to pall. They hadn't discussed it yet, but Sophie had the impression that the recent 24/7 exposure to Marty had exposed some of his frailties to Johnny. As she poured herself a glass, she could hear Johnny singing to Amy as he put her to bed. The way he was with Amy, she still loved him for that and for his other many attributes, not the least being his forgiving nature. Marty was a demonstration of that. The harm he had done to Mary and Johnny by disappearing all those years ago, and Johnny seemed to be able to forgive him for it. She was not sure that she would have been able to do the same had her own father disappeared, but he would never have done that. Her dad, Charles, was too loyal to his wife and to his two daughters. She smiled as she thought of him. Another man who was forgiving to a fault, particularly to her mother, Isabelle. It had been a normal visit when they had dropped into her family home in Rye to pick Amy up. Her father all smiles, pleased to see them and eager to learn how their trip had been, and her mother uninterested in the trip but keen to let them know how their parenting was letting Amy down.

Tough but fair was the way Charles described Isabelle. Sophie had never agreed with him, her view being that her mother was simply tough. Fairness didn't come into it. She agreed with her father on most things, but Isabelle was an exception. She hoped that she was more like Charles when it came to her own personality but secretly feared that she might be more like Isabelle. She knew she could be hard on other people's failings and soft on her own, a trait of her mother's. It made her feel slightly ashamed about cheating on Johnny with Juste, even though nothing much had come of it. She reminded herself, as she always did, of Johnny's infidelities, and that assuaged her guilt a little. Right on cue, he appeared.

'She's asleep, I think, and I'm going to need to be pretty soon, too. I'm fucking knackered. That was a tiring trip back. I guess the all-day hangover didn't help. The other thing that didn't help was Marty's constant dialogue. You wouldn't call him the strong-and-silent type, would you?'

'Well, you like to chat, Johnny. Maybe that's where you get it from?'

Sophie poured Johnny a glass of wine.

'Agreed I like to chat, but I hope I'm not that full on. He's not the world's greatest listener either, is he? I suppose it's my fault for asking him along with us. I'll think a bit harder before I do that again.'

'Maybe it was a long time to spend together when you've only just met.'

'Yeah, you're right. I know I can be a bit impulsive sometimes. I guess inviting Marty was one of those times. It was a great trip all the same, though. Arthur was a fucking hero. I still can't get over the whole naked, flower-on-his-cock thing.'

They both laughed.

'Did you have a good time?'

Sophie felt herself colour a little. 'Yes, I love going to Paris. I loved the exhibition, too.'

'Those friends of yours are live wires, aren't they? Juste is quite something.'

'She certainly is.' Sophie got up and began to busy herself around the kitchen sink. A discussion of Juste's personality traits with Johnny was a little too close for comfort.

As she listened to Johnny snoring gently in bed later, she found herself thinking of Tracey Emin's tent. She closed her eyes and saw Juste, her face close to her own, her eyes big, consuming her, and her mouth on hers. Somehow she didn't feel so much like she was cheating on Johnny because it had been with another woman. She felt as if the tent at *Sensation* had somehow opened her mind to new possibilities. Overall, she was happy with Johnny, and happy with their little family unit, but if she could have other experiences without hurting her family, then she would have them.

***

Mark swilled the whisky around the bottom of his glass and reflected on the trip to Paris. Arthur had decided to go back home to his studio, so he was alone in his Islington flat. He was back to some real work tomorrow, starting an audit at Parsons Warren, the big firm of chartered surveyors in the City. He had managed to pass his time in Paris off as a business trip, despite the fact that he hadn't introduced Arthur to his firm as a client. He had decided to keep the work side of his relationship with Arthur to himself for the moment. Who knew, it might even lead to a change of direction for him if Arthur's success continued. Things had altered so much for him over the past few months – a steady(ish) relationship with Arthur, a new interest in art, some foreign travel – but what he realised was that everything had been kickstarted by the *Sensation* exhibition. He had met Arthur and formed a connection, not least because of the art. He remembered standing in front of the piece by the Chapman Brothers, completely perplexed and slightly appalled by the mass of naked mannequins with misplaced genitals, androgynous and with incongruous Fila trainers on their feet. It had been Arthur who had opened his eyes to a different way of thinking about these images, and really a different way of thinking about art in general. This had led him to a mindset that was much less closed, open to new ideas and experiences. He knew that he was quite a staid person. People were always surprised when they discovered that he was gay; he wasn't a typical gay man. He had understood that. But then Arthur wasn't a typical gay man either. Maybe that was why they got on.

The Paris exhibition really had been quite something. The opening with Arthur's naked form in the spotlight, the slightly ridiculous joke flower squirting yellow water into his mouth, surrounded by his creations, sputtering and whirring as they came to life, this was an experience Mark would never forget. He had come a long way from the slightly stifling semi-detached life he had grown up in. He loved his parents; they were nice, kind people, predictable and unsurprising. This was what he thought he had wanted for himself, but deep down he had known that his sexuality was likely to mean that his life wouldn't be like theirs. It scared him a little the path that he was on, but he wouldn't have it any other way. He felt as if he could be himself around Arthur, which was something new in a relationship for him. The longest time he had spent in a relationship previously was with Victoria, and while he had really liked her, he had known that he was living a lie. He knew the whole time he was with her that he wanted to be with a man. Hence the dalliances with Johnny. He had never been in love with Victoria, but had he been in love with Johnny? Was he still in love with Johnny? If he had been, it had faded. There was no doubt in his mind that he was in love with Arthur. His thoughts were never too far away from him; it was an all-consuming thing. He realised that his feelings were accentuated by Arthur's mystery. He still knew very little about his upbringing or school years; these were just not things that he talked about. He knew he had been to Goldsmiths for his fine art degree and since then had lived at the studio in Shoreditch making his art. He seemed to know most of the other YBAs from his Goldsmiths years, but anything before that was still a mystery to Mark. This enigmatic quality was part of his appeal, Mark understood, but it kept him wanting all the same.

***

Henri pulled on a Disque Bleu and exhaled. He took a sip of his glass of Noilly Prat on the rocks, cold and dry on the palate, the white wine base fortified, a little bitter with a hint of Indian spices. Delicious. He looked around Maison Prunier at the stylish art deco decor and the equally stylish clientele. He felt as if he had chosen the restaurant well. Seafood always seemed romantic to him – well, more than romantic. The physicality of eating shellfish, the rawness, the juices, the use of your hands, all this seemed sensual to him. Once again he had made the effort to arrive early and was waiting for Caroline. He had known that she was in Paris for a couple more nights after the exhibition before returning to Geneva and was glad that he had taken the risk of asking her for dinner. The shark was circling, relentless in the pursuit of his prey. By Geneva standards his status and background growing up had been run of the mill; their house in the suburbs of Coppet on the shores of Lac Léman comfortable but not palatial. Many of his peers at the International School, like Caroline, had been wealthier, better connected and had lived in big houses with swimming pools, and views over the lake. He aspired to that elite caste, and Caroline was a way into it for him.

He stood up smiling as he saw her enter the restaurant. Heads turned as she walked with her statuesque gait towards their table. She wore a round-necked black-and-white checked suit, with the skirt riding several inches above the knee. The jacket was buttoned right up, and she sported an ivory-coloured silk scarf around her long, elegant neck. The suit was undoubtedly by Chanel. He wasn't sure about the scarf. They kissed on each cheek by way of greeting. Henri called the nearest waiter straight over for Caroline to order a drink.

'What would you like to drink, Caroline? I'm just finishing a vermouth, but maybe a glass a champagne.'

'That would be wonderful,' she said, settling into her seat.

'We'll have a bottle of Pol Roger please.' Henri did not want to be seen to be holding back.

'So have you recovered from the exhibition?' he asked.

'It was quite a night, wasn't it? I guess all your English chums are back at home by now.'

'I think so. I haven't bothered anyone today, but we do need to talk about that offer from Édouard. Has he called you?'

'No, not yet.'

'Nor me, but he definitely will soon.'

'You think he was serious?'

'Unquestionably.'

'Did you talk price with him?'

'No, I thought I'd leave that to you, but I'm happy to discuss it. I know he's a client of mine, but I'm on your side.'

'Well, we talked about fifty thousand euros apiece, but that was for individual pieces. Do you think we should discount that for a sale of all seven?'

'No, I don't. I think we should increase it. There must be a premium for a complete collection.'

'Really?'

'Yes, based on the old principle of a pair of something being worth more than two individually. Seven of something must be worth even more.' Henri smiled at Caroline. He looked at her mouth as she spoke, her red lips full, luring him in. She reminded him of Sharon Stone, her blonde hair cut quite short, her athletic build, and that wide mouth.

'Have you had any other interest?' he asked.

'Well, nothing definite, but several people asked me about pricing at the opening. The footfall in the gallery has increased for the last couple of days, too. Did you see *Le Figaro*? There was a brief review, neither particularly positive nor negative, but all publicity is good publicity, right?' She laughed. She had quite a hearty laugh, throwing her head back in a genuine way. She was quite a physical woman, strong and confident, almost manly. It was a quality that Henri found very attractive. He laughed with her.

They ordered their food. Henri suggested some Breton oysters and a piece of turbot to share cooked on the bone with a beurre blanc sauce; Caroline seemed very happy to go with his recommendation. They returned to the subject of *The Seven Deadly Sins*.

'I think we need to aim high with Édouard. If we pitch the price too low he might not think he can make enough money. I know what he's doing. He's trying to get in first with a new artist who he thinks might take off in a big way. He would be looking to make a multiple of his money over the next few years. I think we should start at one million and negotiate down to seven or eight hundred thousand. He will want to negotiate, to feel like he's getting a good price.'

'That would be a fantastic deal for us, and for Arthur. That kind of price for a relative unknown is unusual. It's twice what we wanted.'

'I think you can get it.'

Caroline looked pretty buzzed by the prospect. 'That would be fabulous. It would certainly impress my parents.'

'What did they think of the show? I didn't get the chance to talk to them much.'

'Well, Papa was pretty negative; Maman was more neutral. She is not quite so quick to judge.'

'Why was your dad negative?'

'Well, Papa has grown up dealing in the paintings that have

made European art the world's most famous and valuable art form. If you look at European painters from, say, around 1850 to the Second World War – which would include impressionism, art nouveau, expressionism, cubism and surrealism – then we are talking about the titans of art in the modern world. If you think of the blue-chip artists – like Picasso, Monet, Van Gogh, for example – Papa has lived through a dreamy period for dealing in art. And he has been here in Paris, right at the centre of everything. He's old enough to have met Picasso and to be able to tell his customers that he has. He starts to lose interest when we get to abstract expressionism, although he has sold more than one Jackson Pollock and maybe even a Rothko, but the idea of an artist from the north of England making crazy metal models in a studio in the East End of London just seems quite lowbrow to him.'

'But, snobbery aside, what did he think of them?'

'Well, he was very dismissive of the "performance" side of the opening. He thought some of the pieces had some merit on a fairly basic level, but I think he considers himself to be an aesthete, and he couldn't see any aesthetic merit in the work.'

'Do you agree with him?'

'That's a big question. I don't think of art in the same way as him. I don't think a work of art has to be a painting or a sculpture. I think the possibilities are much broader. That's not a new idea, obviously. I believe Arthur's work makes you think. I also find it very funny, which has to be a good thing.'

'Do you think it's supposed to be funny?'

'Of course, I do. He's a funny guy. He's cocking a snook at authority. I think all the YBAs are doing this, some in more obvious ways than others.'

'Do you think people will still be looking at this stuff in a hundred years' time?'

'Personally, yes I do.'

'So, personally, would you rather spend time looking at *The*

Narcissist, or would you rather be sitting in front of one of Monet's *Water Lilies*.'

'I think there's a time and place for both.' Henri smiled at Caroline, he smiled and simultaneously looked into her eyes, and perhaps for the first time since their school days he felt a connection as she smiled and looked directly back at him. The arrival of the oysters interrupted them. Half a dozen plump Bretons were placed in front of each of them, their half-shells on a plate of ice decorated with seaweed. The smell alone was sensational: iodine and sea salt. Henri lost no time in lifting up the first shell with his left hand while using the small fork in his right to release the oyster from the adductor muscle that still held it to its shell. He then poured the entire contents of the shell into his mouth. For him, eating an oyster was as much about texture as taste; he bit into the soft creamy texture of the body of the mollusc before the salty liquid in the bottom of the shell washed it all down. He felt an immediate rush, almost like an overdose of minerality. A quick sip of Pol Roger, and he was ready for the next.

'So, what do you think of Arthur's work?' she asked him.

'Well, I wouldn't have it in my house. I think I'm more of an old-school aesthete like your dad when it comes to art – as I told you, I was very taken by the shark in formaldehyde last year. Did you see it?' He downed another oyster as he finished speaking. He watched as Caroline did the same. She seemed to be enjoying them in as physical a way as he was.

'Yes, I think Damien Hirst is going to be huge.'

'I still think about that piece. That must be a sign that it's had an impact of some kind.'

'I can see why you like it. It suits you!' Caroline laughed again, tossing her head back. Henri wasn't used to being teased like this by a woman – by anyone, for that matter. He wasn't sure how he felt, but he decided to laugh along anyway. They went back to chatting about the deal, finishing the oysters as they spoke. Henri realised that he would have to be on his toes when it came to Caroline. He liked to feel like he was always slightly ahead in a relationship, and he normally managed it with ease, but she was very smart, perhaps smarter than him. He would have to stay ahead by using his guile and finding her weak spots. She had already opened up far more than usual this evening. He knew that she was staying with her parents in Paris – which probably meant she wouldn't want to stay over with him at his flat tonight. Never mind. He would save that for another time. He would flirt a little, be as charming as he could and maybe kiss her at the end of the evening, just to make sure that she understood how he felt. He looked forward to it, as the creamy, salty taste of the last of the oysters filled his mouth and a little of the juice ran down his chin. He quickly wiped this away with a napkin. Caroline was watching him, her mouth slightly open, smiling.

SUMMER

1998

'Shall we try that again? I'm still not happy.'

Johnny got a thumbs-up from his producer Damian. Marty, seated next to Damian, gave a second thumbs-up. Johnny had been lucky to be able to talk Damian Harris into helping him put his new album together. Damian was the founder of Skint Records and more of a dance-music man. In fact, in league with Norman Cook, he had almost single-handedly created the big beat sound down in Brighton over the previous couple of years. Johnny was interested in trying to take the sound of his new band more in this direction. He had loved *Screamadelica* by Primal Scream when it had come out; the idea of fusing an indie-guitar-based sound with a dance-influenced backing track had stayed with him. Damian had played him Norman Cook's latest recordings, which were shortly to be released as an album. The single 'The Rockafeller Skank', just pre-released before the album, was already a huge hit and had become one of the sounds of the summer. Johnny thought what he'd heard of the rest of the album was just as good. It had convinced him to try to pin Damian down to work with him on 'Dead Dad' and the rest of his new material. Fortunately, Damian had agreed, and here they were in his small recording studio in Brighton, only an hour or so from home for Johnny. Rightly or wrongly, he had taken Marty on as a general factotum for the duration of the recording. Having a driver meant he could load up in the studio when the fancy took him and still get home each night, however late it was. The downside was that Marty had become a self-appointed assistant producer. He could tell that Damian's patience was wearing thin on this front; an assistant grounded in early-seventies pub rock was not what he needed. Slightly more manageable were Dave and Rob, who had loyally stayed with Johnny for the recording sessions, although Rob's speed intake was having a negative effect on his own attempts to stay sober.

'OK, let's go from the intro.'

Johnny was trying to lay down a heavily wah-wahed guitar lick over the first few bars of 'Dead Dad'. The song had changed almost beyond recognition since he had played the acoustic version at the Powerhaus; there was now an intro led by a heavy drumbeat supplied by Dave, a deep bass provided by Rob, and some soulful brass supplied by Damian's box of tricks. Johnny was overlaying that with some Hendrix-influenced wah-wah. They weren't yet sure if this was going to work. He tried to relax and let the music wash over him as he listened through his headphones. He wanted his playing to be more instinctive, a reaction to the sound around him. He tried again and lost himself in his playing for fifteen seconds or so until the opening bars finished and his recorded vocals began. He stopped playing. That had been closer to what he had wanted. He looked at Damian through the window to the control room and was met with a broad grin and a thumbs-up.

'Nailed it,' he heard through the headphones.

Even Marty was smiling.

Later, as they drove back to the house in Brede, Johnny felt himself zoning out as Marty chuntered away about the day's recording.

'I thought your playing was better today, Johnny. Somehow you seemed to be able to bring a bit more soul to it.'

'Thanks, Marty.'

Johnny sat in the passenger seat with his eyes closed. He was looking forward to seeing Sophie and Amy. They hadn't finished that late at the studio today, so Amy would still be up when they got home. Having Marty staying was difficult for Sophie; not just because she didn't particularly like him but his presence at the house meant that Johnny's mother was no longer available to help with Amy, unless they took her over to Mary's flat in St Leonards. Mary had made it clear that an encounter with Marty was out of the question.

'I'm not sure if I mentioned it, but I met Charles Pitts when I was in the States. Lovely man. He played the wah-wah guitar on the 'Theme from Shaft'. I wonder if we should be thinking about sampling that on the intro to 'Dead Dad' instead of using your part. That might work, you know. Worth a discussion, I would have thought.'

Johnny pretended to be asleep. He tried to be patient with Marty, but he was not an easy guy. He had opinions on all subjects. He wasn't offended by the suggestion of using someone else's guitar intro, just a bit tired of Marty's constant intrusions. Johnny had suggested to Sophie that they use him to babysit Amy while he was staying with them. He felt like he and Sophie didn't get enough time on their own at the best of times; now that Marty was around he could help them out a little. Sophie was totally against the idea; she just didn't trust Marty – certainly not enough to be left alone with their daughter. Johnny hadn't managed to establish whether or not this was because of past or present misdemeanours or just an intuitive assessment of Marty's character. Whatever the case, the potential upsides to having Marty on the scene were dwindling.

'There's an art to wah-wah. I think the older guitarists from the sixties and seventies understood it better. Hendrix, Jeff Beck, Clapton. All wonderful wah-wah players, too. Charles Pitts was the master, though, and such a lovely guy.'

They might be working in Brighton for at least another month.

Johnny was going to have to seriously consider whether or not he could put up with Marty for that long.

'By the way, son. There's something I've been meaning to ask you. This Marty thing. You always call me Marty. I thought you would have called me Dad. I'm not too worried either way, but think about it. Amy calls me Grandad; it seems a bit funny that you don't call me Dad. I'll leave it with you anyway.'

Johnny carried on pretending to be asleep. Marty would have to earn his stripes if he wanted to be called Dad. As things currently stood, he was a long way from qualifying.

***

Caroline had asked him to come and see her in Geneva, and he had come running. He felt like he had seemed a little too eager. He sipped on his small *pression* and inhaled a lungful of smoke from a Disque Bleu. The last of the evening sun dappled his tanned face and his crisp white Lanvin shirt. His eyes were protected from the glare by metal-framed, retro-looking Gucci sunglasses, and his feet were provided comfort and style by Gucci loafers. He felt good. He admitted to himself that he was excited to be seeing Caroline, and he had made the extra effort with his appearance to impress her. While he hadn't seen her in the flesh for a couple of months because of their travel schedules, they had had lots of phone contact. The deal with Édouard had been completed, at just under a million euros, and everyone had been paid. They had done a good job of publicising the sale of all *Seven Deadly Sins* to a single collector, with Édouard's blessing, and now Arthur Swale was hot property. Ostensibly it was the next step in Arthur's career that they were here to talk about, but he had an inkling that there might be more than one reason for Caroline's invitation. He would wait and see how the night panned out.

He felt comfortably familiar at his table on the terrace at La Clémence, surrounded by louche-looking Genevois drinkers, with some of whom he was on nodding terms, alumni of the International School, fellow bankers, a pool of fledgling Geneva movers and shakers relaxing after a day of talking up their books. As ever, he was early for his appointment, ensuring that he was properly installed before Caroline arrived, relaxed and ready to do conversational battle. He knew that Caroline lived in a flat on her own in the Old Town, a short walk away down the cobbled medieval streets from where he was sitting in Place du Bourg-de-Four. He had positioned himself on the terrace so that he could see her before she saw him, and suddenly there she was, less formally dressed than usual in low-cut hipster jeans and a tight-cropped, white-ribbed vest, maybe Gucci as well. She, too, wore sunglasses, which Henri identified as Versace, even at a distance, as the large gold logo between the lenses and the arms glinted in the sun. She walked slowly and elegantly but purposefully, swaying a little from side to side. She saw him and immediately waved, smiling. She seemed genuinely pleased to see him. He stood at the table as she approached and touched her bare arms as he kissed her on both cheeks. Her skin felt warm to the touch.

'Thanks so much for coming at such short notice. I wanted to share my news with you before I talk to Arthur and Mark. I could have told you on the phone, but I thought it might be much more fun to celebrate in person.'

This was unusually effusive for Caroline. She was normally quite measured.

'Does it call for champagne?'

'Most definitely.'

The waiter had already approached, and Henri ordered a bottle of Moët & Chandon.

Henri kept his cool outwardly but was inwardly desperate to learn what had made Caroline so animated.

'So, there are two pieces of news. The first is that I have decided, with my parents' backing, to open a gallery in London. In Hoxton to be precise. I'm so pleased that they are prepared to back me, but after the success of Arthur's show in Paris, even my father has been convinced. I'm still not sure that he likes the art, but he's a businessman at heart, and he can see that if we want to be a big part of the contemporary art scene we need to be in London as well as in Paris. Probably New York, too, but London is a good start.'

'Wow, that *is* a big deal.'

'Yes, isn't it amazing? And it's because of you, Henri. That's where it all started. I couldn't be happier.'

The champagne arrived, and they clinked their glasses across the small table. As they did so Caroline leaned forward and, to his great surprise, kissed him on the mouth. He was shocked into silence, so he diverted the attention from his shock by fumbling for a Disque Bleu and lighting it.

'I think I've wanted to do that for a while, Henri. I hope you don't mind.'

He waited a moment to exhale the smoke. It gave him the chance to collect himself. 'I definitely don't mind.' He squeezed her hand as it lay on the table. She smiled straight into his eyes as he did so, and he felt the electricity both from her touch and her gaze. He moved his hand away gently, not wanting to be too pushy. 'I have a vague recollection that we kissed when we were at school. Do you remember that?' He looked straight at her as he asked. He had assumed that she had forgotten, as she had never mentioned it.

'You know, now you mention it, I do remember. Was it at a party, by someone's pool?'

'Yes, it was. It was at Arnaud's place. In Cologny.'

'That's right. I remember.'

'I wonder why it only happened the once.' Henri wanted to see how she responded.

'Now *that* I don't remember.' This was a white lie. Henri could tell by the way she looked down at the table as she said it. 'But that doesn't matter now that we have reconnected, does it?' She raised her eyes and looked back at him. The look felt like an invitation. He would find out later if it was. He realised that Caroline was in control of the situation, not him, and, while this was unusual, he was prepared to go along with it.

'Anyway, back to business,' she continued. 'The second piece of news is just as exciting. Have you heard of Harald Szeemann?'

'No, I don't recognise the name.'

'Well, he's from Zurich, very influential in the art world, not just in Switzerland but everywhere. He's the curator of next year's Venice Biennale.'

'And how does that affect us?'

'My parents are very good friends with him. As soon as I heard about his appointment I suggested they get in touch. I know that he loves to give young, contemporary artists a chance. Who better to represent Great Britain at the Biennale than Arthur Swale? They've spoken to Harald, and he loves the idea. He knew all about our exhibition in Paris, and he's already spoken to the team in London that chooses the British artist. They love the idea, too. Arthur Swale is going to Venice!'

'Wow, that's incredible.' Henri was genuinely taken aback by this news. 'Does he know yet?

'No, but we should be able to tell him in a couple of weeks. I think that's worth another kiss.'

She leaned over and kissed him again on the mouth, this time a little harder and for a little longer.

'I think we should finish the champagne, forget dinner and go back to my apartment. How does that sound?'

'That sounds like a perfect evening,' he said.

A little later they left the bar and set off down Rue de l'Hôtel de Ville. She took his hand in hers, and he felt the electricity of her touch once more. He wondered if she felt the same. It was a short walk to Rue des Granges and her apartment in one of Geneva's most prestigious streets. They hurried through the large entrance and almost ran up the stone stairway to the first floor. She fumbled in her bag for the keys and opened the front door, laughing to herself. She closed the door behind them firmly and pushed him against the wall, kissing him again hard on the mouth, her hands pulling his shirt from his trousers. He pushed back against her and began to pull up her vest, but she pushed him back against the wall. She was physically strong, not as strong as him but much stronger than other women in his experience. There was no doubting her femininity, but he could feel masculinity in the way she behaved. For the first time in his life he felt like he was being dominated sexually. She took his hand and directed him to her bedroom where she pushed him on to the bed.

Later, when she had finished with him and lay next to him breathing softly as she slept, he reflected on what had happened. He was in no doubt that he had enjoyed the last couple of hours, but he had not been in charge. Caroline had spent a lot of time on top of him with her eyes closed, moving slowly up and down on him; he had loved looking at her beautiful naked body as she did so, watching her move, looking at her face and her expressions of pleasure, but at the same time he had felt almost used. When he had tried to touch her breasts as she moved, she had silently and firmly moved his arms back to his sides, almost pinning him down. In many ways this feeling of being dominated was against everything he believed about himself. Henri – the shark, the dominant player at the poker table, the cunning negotiator, the winner, a man who liked to think he was always one step ahead – controlled in bed by a woman. It was difficult to come to terms with; nonetheless he admitted to himself that a part of him had loved it and found it highly erotic. In the end he had given in; he had kissed back when she wanted to kiss him, he had given her cunnilingus when she had pushed his head in that direction and he had let her touch him wherever and however she wanted. When he had sexually fantasised about Caroline he had been the dominant partner, but the reality had proved to be entirely different. His life had never been very contradictory until now; it had been about certainty. Sure, there had been the odd hiccup in business, but in his relationships, both personal and professional, he had felt in control. It was not like that with Caroline. Uncertainty was not a subject that he had ever dwelled on before, and he felt unusually troubled. He turned on to his side and put his arm around Caroline's naked body as she slept with her back to him. She had almost behaved as if she had just had a workout at the gym; once she had finished with him she had kissed him on the mouth, turned on to her side and within seconds had begun to snore very softly. No post-coital conversation, no asking him what he was thinking, not even a visit to the bathroom. To his surprise, he admired her for it. He decided not to ponder any further the whys and wherefores of what had just occurred; he at least felt physically tired and sexually satisfied. It was not like him to feel this kind of mental weakness. He needed to take what had happened for what it was, a new experience, and one that he had enjoyed. He smelled Caroline's fragrance as she slept, and it relaxed him. If this was how his relationship with her was going to be, then he would rather have the relationship than not have it.

***

Sophie added some crushed dried chilli to the onions and garlic she had started frying, then a teaspoon each of garam masala, coriander, cumin and turmeric. She had browned some cubed lamb neck and would add that just after some tomatoes and peppers once the onions and spices had cooked off a little more. Johnny was due back from his last recording session in Brighton, which had meant that his irritating father had finally been packed off on a train back to London. Johnny was due home alone by car shortly, so she wanted to finish the curry and get Amy to bed before he arrived. She sipped on a glass of Chenin blanc while she stirred the pan. As she was cooking she had been trying to work out if she had a crush on Juste or if it was something more serious. Their clinch in Paris was never too far from her mind. She had decided that the only way to work that out was to see her again, this time on her own turf, so she had hatched a plan to lure Juste to visit her shop in Rye and stay at least a night at the house in Brede. She knew that Véronique would have to stay in Paris to mind their own shop. Ideally Juste's trip to England would coincide with Johnny being away. She was quite happy with Johnny, and she still felt like she loved him, despite the past, but she needed more. She knew that many people would think of this as morally suspect, but, while she did not miss Henri, she missed the excitement her relationship with him had created. The anticipation of seeing Juste gave her that same feeling.

At that moment she heard Johnny pull up outside the house. It was so quiet where they were in the Brede Valley that noise carried quickly, and, right on cue, she heard Amy exclaim 'Daddy!' and run to open the front door. She knew that he would be as excited to see Amy as she was to see him. She waited a while before he stuck his head around the door to greet her.

'Something smells good.'

'Lamb curry. If you put Amy to bed we can enjoy it in peace.' She smiled at him, and he smiled back.

The curry was ready by the time he came downstairs. She poured him a glass of the white wine and they sat down at the kitchen table.

'Man, it's good to be on our own.'

'Yes. I take it the third wheel is safely back in London.'

'I assume so.'

'It's been hard going, hasn't it?'

'Yes, I know. But once I'd asked him I didn't think I could go back on it.'

'Two months of Marty has been a little like Chinese water

torture. The drip-drip of a combination of conceit and cynicism. He's not wrong about much, is he?'

'Imagine that in the studio? I'm surprised Damian stayed the distance.'

'He was lovely with Amy once they got to know each other.'

'Yes, he was. And it was good for me, too. I feel like I know him much better now. Warts and all. It'll be good to take a break from him, though. You know what he's doing next?'

'Going back to being a jobbing guitarist?'

'No. He's going to be Arthur Swale's assistant.'

'Seriously?'

'I know. I couldn't believe it either. You remember Caroline Schmidt?'

'Yes, of course.'

'She's opening a new gallery in Shoreditch. I'm surprised Mark hadn't told me, but I haven't spoken to him for a while. Anyway, Arthur is doing a couple of pieces for the opening night. I'm sure we'll get an invite. It's coming up in a month or so, I think.'

'How strange about Marty.'

'I know. He slated Arthur's stuff in Paris. They must have connected on some level or other, though.'

***

Mark sat in the Baring Arms nursing a pint of Guinness, waiting for Arthur. Mark was not sure he liked the pub that much, but he wanted to see Arthur, and Arthur liked its authenticity. Mark felt conspicuous in his suit, which he was still wearing, as he was on his way home from work. The other customers were real Londoners, East Enders even, as the pub was on the fringes of East London here, only a couple of miles northeast of Bethnal Green, which was almost at the centre of the area that was generally accepted as being the home of the authentic cockney. There were only a handful of men at the bar, it being a quiet Tuesday evening.

They were a youngish group, probably Mark's age, around thirty, dressed in designer jeans and trainers, bragging and ribbing each other in that overconfident way of young men that often belies a lack of confidence. As the evening wore on a few regulars would come in after the evening meals they had taken at home. These men tended to be older, in their forties and fifties. Less vocal and a little more threatening. He had noticed on previous visits that every now and again a couple of the older ones would go off to the gents together and come back quite a long time later. At first, he had thought they were cottaging, as unlikely as that kind of gay behaviour might seem in a very blokey East End pub. Having dismissed the idea, he then wondered if maybe it was drugs. He had discovered the truth by accident on a previous occasion when he had visited the loo and had overheard a conversation going on inside before he entered. He had frozen at the entrance, not wanting to be accused of listening in on something he should not have been listening in on but unable to go back to his seat without relieving himself. From what he heard it became apparent that the couples were visiting the gents to discreetly discuss criminal activity. He had overheard a snippet of a low-voiced conversation about a warehouse burglary. Since then he had made sure he did not interrupt any of these clandestine meetings by keeping a regular eye on the comings and goings, timing his own visits to avoid any unwanted eavesdropping. At that moment Arthur arrived, bursting through the door in his usual flurry of unkempt hair and rapid-action, black-clothed limbs. Mark felt himself smile as he saw him. He walked straight to the bar then turned to Mark.

'Do you want another Guinness, Mark?'

It was typical of him not even to say hello. Public displays of affection were definitely also out, although they were for Mark, too, in a place like the Baring Arms.

'No thanks.'

Arthur ordered a lager and sat down. 'Fuck me. I'm knackered, mate. I'm not sure how many of these openings I can take.'

'I thought this one was smaller than Paris?'

'Well, it is, but it's always a fuckin' rush at the end. I'm glad to get out for a pint. I let Marty off early, too. He's been surprisingly useful.'

'Johnny called me the other night. He's quite pleased you've given Marty something to do. He was driving him nuts at the recording studio.'

'Well, he drives me nuts if I listen, but I don't fuckin' listen.' Arthur grinned at Mark. 'He's quite good at following directions, and he's good with his hands. Anyway, we're nearly there. It's just a couple of pieces. I've decided *The Narcissist* was to be the first in a series of personality disorders. The next two are *The Obsessive Compulsive* and *The Paranoiac*. They're just about finished.'

It was unusual for Arthur to discuss his art with Mark. However, more recently he had occasionally talked about what he was doing, not in any detail, but, even so, Mark took it as a sign that he trusted him more and more. While not a paranoiac, Arthur's starting point in his dealings with other human beings was one of absolute distrust.

'Johnny's coming to the opening, by the way. Sophie is minding Amy so staying at home. I think she also has someone over from France. Johnny will probably stay with me that night.' Arthur ignored these details. He was never very interested in the comings and goings of Mark's friends.

'Henri tells me they're going to announce me for the Biennale at the opening. He dropped by the studio with Caroline yesterday on a flying visit to check out the art.' Mark was never encouraged to drop into the studio, so this pissed him off a little. 'They seemed to like the new pieces. We're borrowing *The Narcissist* again, too, so it should look good with all three of them there.'

'That's very exciting about the Biennale. Fame at last, eh?'

'I don't know about that. Some fucker from the British Council's coming, so they say. I'll have to come up with something good for Venice. I'm thinking about including more performance art. I've been reading a book about Houdini, and it's got me thinking.'

Mark felt his stomach tense up at the mention of Houdini; he had thought Paris would be hard to beat when it came to performance art.

Arthur continued. 'It had never occurred to me before, but it seems obvious now that Houdini was an artist, a performance artist. I don't think he gets the recognition he deserves. Some of the stuff he got up to was mind blowing. He was pretty obsessed with death. His brother and his father died prematurely when he was quite young. This might be the explanation for why he genuinely took potentially mortal risks in his performances.'

Shit, thought Mark, what is he planning? 'I'm afraid I don't know much about Houdini. It all sounds a bit macabre, though.'

'Death is the one certainty in all our lives, Mark. We need to embrace it, not fear it.'

Mark felt himself shiver slightly, grabbed his pint and took a long draught.

***

Caroline had changed and was now in the hotel bathroom putting on her make-up. A few minutes earlier they had finished a rapid and slightly brutal sex act. Caroline, as was her custom, had been moving up and down on top of him, and he had unconsciously moved one of his hands from his side to try to touch her breasts. She had pushed his arm back to his side quite forcefully and then slapped him hard across the face. After this she had continued to move up and down on him quicker and quicker, her hands pushing forcefully down on his chest, bringing them both rapidly to orgasm. At the time it had felt quite erotic. Now, a few minutes later, as he lay alone in bed, he felt very different. His face still stung from the slap, but the damage to his ego was much greater. He felt humiliated and confused. Caroline came out of the bathroom and sat on the side of the bed. She touched his face gently where she had slapped him.

'Well, there's nothing showing. We wouldn't want you to have a red mark on your face for the opening. I'm sorry, I got a little carried away there. You seem to like it, too, though? It's just a game, right?'

Henri was confused. The switch from sadistic to gentle had happened too rapidly for him to keep up.

'Yes, I liked it, too. Maybe the slap was a little hard, but I liked it.' He wasn't sure why he had lied.

'Come on. You need to dress. I want you looking handsome for my customers. Will you wear a tie for me? It looks so much smarter.'

'Sure, I was going to anyway. I brought the blue Hermès that you like.'

'Perfect. How do I look?'

'Wonderful, as always.' She really did look wonderful. She was wearing one of her collection of little black dresses – he thought it was the Chanel – with sheer black stockings and patent black pumps. Despite himself, he thought she looked entrancing.

'Right, you have five minutes, then we need to be in a cab to the gallery. That will have us arriving around one hour before the guests. I want to be there before Papa and Maman. They told me they will be half an hour early.'

Henri was already out of bed and washing quickly in the sink.

'How do you think our artist is going to behave tonight?' Caroline asked.

'I think he'll have something up his sleeve.'

'What do you think of the new pieces?'

'They're not quite as impressive as *The Seven Deadly Sins*, but he had less time. I do think they work well as a continuation of the theme he introduced with *The Narcissist*. It really helps that you were able to borrow that again. The two new works on their own wouldn't be as powerful.'

'Yes, I agree. I think we have enough for the opening, but only just. I hope he's not running out of steam.'

'Well, he has some help now, from Marty.'

'Yes, Marty. He's quite opinionated, given he's supposed to be an assistant. I hope he's not influencing Arthur too much.'

'You know he's Johnny Jones's father?'

'Yes, I remember from Paris.'

'I agree he's opinionated, but I don't think Arthur takes any notice. The important thing is that Arthur produces more art. That would be good for everyone.'

By now Henri was buttoning his shirt and tying his tie. Almost ready for the fray. He put the slap to the back of his mind. He needed to be at his most confident best tonight, working the room as he believed only he could.

***

Mark was always a little apprehensive before any social gathering, but he found Arthur's exhibitions particularly nerve-racking. He seemed to worry about them more than Arthur did. He had decided to meet Johnny beforehand for a couple of pints of Dutch courage before the official opening tonight, and his cab was approaching the pub they had chosen. Mark thought Caroline was taking a bit of a risk opening the gallery in Hoxton, but Arthur, Henri and some other dealer contacts of Caroline's had convinced her that her timing was perfect; she was at the start of a wave of contemporary galleries that were likely to appear in Hoxton and Shoreditch over the next couple of years. Caroline had been so convinced this would happen that, with her parents' backing, she had bought a spacious industrial building on the western side of the square. Mark had helped with the financial side of the transaction as well as with recommendations for the fit-out. Everything had been done at breakneck speed, and now they were ready to open Galerie Schmidt London only a year or so after the *Sensation* exhibition at the Royal Academy.

The Royal Oak in Columbia Road, which Johnny always described as a 'proper boozer', was a short walk away from Hoxton Square. On a recent weekend visit to the flower market in the street outside the pub, Mark had dropped in for a quick pint and had been comforted to see cubes of cheddar cheese and crackers for free on the bar here on a Sunday lunchtime. It reminded him of his recent youth, back in the eighties, before the licensing laws changed, when pub Sunday lunchtimes were an express-paced drinking session that lasted only two hours. He was pretty sure that he had introduced Johnny to the Royal Oak when he was a student at UCL. He was sure he had also originally come here with Sophie when they had discovered the flower market and bought some pot plants for their flat in Wapping. It seemed like a long time ago. He had carried a torch for Sophie back then; he was so pleased that he felt so much more confident about his sexuality now. Despite Arthur's foibles, he was as happy as he'd ever been in a relationship. As the cab arrived at the pub, he admired its familiar tiled exterior on the way in and began to look for Johnny. It was busy on a Thursday evening, always a big night in London before commuters and second homers left for the weekend. He spotted Johnny at the bar, puffing on a Marlboro Light. He had swapped his customary leather jacket for a Crombie and was sporting a pair of retro-looking metal framed sunglasses. Mark always thought Johnny looked cool, but to him at that moment he seemed cooler than ever. He tapped him on the shoulder, and Johnny turned around sharply.

'Arnold, you wanker! What did I tell you, a proper fucking boozer.'

Mark thought Johnny was slightly overplaying the London geezer thing but let it go. 'Hello, Jones,' he said and gave him a hug.

He ordered a couple more drinks, and they found a corner where it was a little quieter.

'So, mate, another big night for the boyfriend. What can I expect?'

Mark realised that Johnny had already had either a few drinks or a line of coke, or both. He recognised the signs of over-refreshment, a slightly exaggerated boisterousness. Johnny was out on the town without his wife so had obviously decided to push the boat out.

'I haven't seen the new art, but Arthur seems excited about it. He seems happy with Marty, too.'

'Well, he's only been doing it for a few weeks, but I haven't heard a peep from him, so Arthur must be keeping him busy. To be honest, that's a good thing. We ended up seeing a bit too much of each other when we were recording.'

'Thanks so much for sending me a CD of the new album, by the way. I love it. It's kind of like Swerve meets the dancefloor.'

'And that's a good thing?'

'I think it is.'

'Damian is really pleased with it.'

'Damian?'

'Yes, Damian Harris from Skint Records. I thought I told you. The guy who just put out Fat Boy Slim's album.'

'Right, of course. That album's brilliant.'

'Well, we're releasing mine as soon as we can. We're hoping to ride the wave. They're calling it big beat, although my stuff is more of a hybrid. As soon as I have an album to sell I'm out on the road.'

'That's fantastic news. Well done, mate.'

'Thanks.'

'Would it be worth me meeting Damian, I mean from a business point of view?'

'Well, I can set it up, but he's more of a music guy than a business guy. How's your work going anyway?'

'I'm a partner now, so there's an expectation that I bring work into the firm. Sorry, I don't want that to get in the way of things.'

'No worries, mate, we've all got to earn a crust.'

'Yes, but that was a bit gauche. Sorry.' Mark took a sip of his drink. Johnny was pretty relaxed about this kind of thing, but that had been a rebuff, and he felt a little embarrassed. He knew their two worlds were very different, and he normally knew to be a little more subtle in how he asked for these kinds of introductions.

He changed the subject. 'By the way, have you heard of the Venice Biennale?'

'Isn't that some kind of art show?'

'Quite right, I'd never heard of it. Well, who do you think has been chosen to represent the UK next year?'

'You're joking . . . Not Arthur fucking Swale?'

'Yes, I know. It's quite surprising, isn't it? There's an official announcement at the opening tonight.'

'Well, bugger me blind, as my grandad used to say. That is a surprise.'

'Make a note in your diary. April 1999. I'm sure Sophie would like to go to Venice.'

'Sounds fantastic. I'll bear it in mind when we're planning the European leg of the tour.'

***

Sophie had left Juste downstairs while she put Amy to bed.

'I like your friend, Mummy. Do you think she would read me a story?'

'Well, I don't know. The easiest way to find out would be to ask her. I'll go and see what I can do.'

Sophie went back down to the kitchen and found Juste warming her feet on the Aga while sat in one of their rustic wooden chairs. She looked at little out of place in the countryside in her ripped jeans and leather bodice. Sophie smiled to herself. She had no plan for their couple of days together and no definitive expectation.

However, somehow the fact that Juste was not in her natural environment had shifted the power base in their relationship.

'Amy has made a request. She would like you to read her bedtime story. Is that OK?'

'It would be an honour! I will go and do my duty.'

Juste got up. She was petite anyway, but without her big boots she looked almost girlish herself. Sophie spontaneously kissed her on the cheek, and she smiled back appreciatively.

'I'll be back. I cannot keep my little princess waiting.' Juste trotted up the stairs to find Amy.

Sophie had picked Juste up earlier that day from Ashford International. She had engineered her visit to coincide with the same evening that Johnny was in London at the gallery opening. Although she had not specifically told Juste that Johnny would not be there, it was implicit. She was sure that Juste would have known that they would be alone, otherwise she would never have come. They had then spent the afternoon at the shop in Rye. She got the sense that Juste had been impressed with the clothes she had in stock and the decor of the shop. Sophie was quite proud of what she had built up over the last few years. Juste had been pleasant but not overfamiliar with her while they were there, complimenting her on her choices. Customers had been coming and going, so it had not been the environment for an intimate discussion. She had the impression that they were both holding back a little, both a little alien to one another after a while apart. Now that they were back home in Brede, in her cosy old farmhouse, things felt a little more intimate. Juste seemed more relaxed this evening; it was not like her to hide her feelings, and now that they were alone it was an opportunity for their conversation to take a more personal turn. While Juste was upstairs Sophie opened a bottle of Chablis, poured herself a glass and started to prepare the moules marinière that she hoped Juste would enjoy. The mussels were local and very fresh. She sang along to the radio as she cleaned the mussels at the sink.

It was Mark Goodier's Radio 1 evening show, and he was playing 'Brimful of Asha' by Cornershop. She loved that song. Once she had finished the mussels she chopped an onion very finely, together with a clove of garlic and a crushed dried chilli before dropping them all into hot olive oil in a saucepan on the Aga. As she stirred this mixture she suddenly felt two hands around her waist; it was Juste, clearly feeling more comfortable, as she pulled Sophie in towards her and nuzzled her neck.

'*Tu sens bien, ma belle*,' she whispered in her ear. Sophie shuddered pleasingly at the sensation of the whispers in her ear. She put her spoon down and turned around to face Juste. Juste kissed her softly on the mouth.

'You smell wonderful, too. What is that perfume?' Sophie asked, smiling.

'Acqua di Gio by Armani. Do you think it suits me?'

'Oh yes! It's totally Eurotrash.' She pushed Juste away laughing. 'Right, now I have to cook the mussels!'

She poured a glass of Chablis into the pan, let it boil down a little then added the mussels and put on the lid. By the time she had poured Juste a glass of wine and laid the table, the mussels were ready. She put the saucepan on the table and took off her apron. She was wearing a short T-shirt and hipster jeans, revealing a little midriff between the two. Her stomach was, she felt, still flat enough to get away with it. She caught Juste looking at the bare skin and smiled at her as she sat down opposite her. She ladled some mussels into a bowl for Juste and passed it over before doing the same for herself. Juste smelled the aroma of the dish.

'So, you can cook, *ma puce*,' Juste said.

'I do my best.'

Juste tried one of the plump mussels, picking it from its shell with a fork. 'Delicious. They're perfect.'

'Thank you.'

'So where is your rock star tonight?'

'He's at the opening of Caroline Schmidt's new gallery.'

'Ah yes, Caroline.'

'She and Henri le Cerf seem to be a couple these days.'

'Yes, I have seen them in Paris occasionally. They're not really my crowd. He seems to be her – how do you say? – poodle.'

'Really?'

'The last time I saw them was in a bar in Madeleine, and all the body language was telling me that she was the boss.'

'That's not like Henri.'

'Well, you would know, *ma chère*.'

'Looking back, I think it was revenge for what Johnny had put me through with Mark.'

'Of course,' Juste extravagantly simulated a blow job with her tongue in the side of her mouth. They both laughed uproariously.

'Yes, revenge for that.'

'Well, at least now you can laugh about it.'

'I think that's the first time, as a matter of fact.'

'So, who am I revenge for?'

'You're not revenge. I think I've got past that. I love Johnny, but, for me, it's not enough. I don't think it's enough for him either. We don't discuss it, but I can feel it. Some art I saw at an exhibition last year opened my eyes to the way that we love. I now think we can love in many different ways and that includes a woman loving another woman. I told Johnny that you were coming, by the way. I'm not sure if he realises that there is something between us. I'm not sure he even cares. He's not the jealous type.'

'Aha. You think there is something between us?'

'Yes, I know there is.'

They held hands across the table, and Juste looked deeply into her eyes, smiling as she did so. Whatever it was between them, she was not sure yet how deep it ran, but there was definitely something.

Later they lay in bed. Sex with Juste had seemed very natural. Sophie did not feel that it had been better than sex with a man, just not the same. Her time with Juste had a different quality of intimacy to the time she spent with Johnny. It felt more intense somehow; she felt lonely sometimes, not only when Johnny was away but even when they were together; she felt none of that loneliness when she was with Juste.

'So, *mon amour*, am I your first woman?'

'Yes, you are.'

'And how was it for you?' Juste said, laughing.

'It was wonderful.'

'Good. I am pleased.'

It seemed easier to have this discussion with a woman. They lay quietly for a while.

'You know, I can never leave Véronique. She needs me. I have to be with her to protect her from the bad stuff in her past.'

Sophie was slightly taken aback. 'I think I realise that. Don't worry. I'm not asking for anything from you other than to enjoy your company from time to time.'

There was a small voice at the door and the shadow of a young girl holding a teddy.

'Mummy, can I get in your bed. I had a bad dream.'

'Of course you can.'

'What is Juste doing here? I thought she was sleeping in the guest room?'

'Well, I had a bad dream, too, *mon amour*, and your mummy let me come into her bed as well.'

As Amy got in between them and Juste fussed over her, Sophie smiled to herself and thought of Tracey Emin's tent. *Everyone I Have Ever Slept With.*

***

The walk from Columbia Road to Hoxton Square only took them a few minutes through the north-eastern hinterland of the City of London. The grungy-looking streets with their mixture of residential blocks, industrial buildings and low-end shops were a counterbalance to the huge City buildings that towered to the south. Johnny was buzzed from the beer and the anticipation of another Swale event. He also surprised himself by realising that he was looking forward to seeing Marty; maybe some kind of paternal bond was developing. They arrived in Hoxton Square, which, at first glance, seemed an unlikely place to be on the cusp of an art revolution. It was quiet, with a garden in the middle and a mix of residential and old industrial buildings around its four sides. Some of these had already become fledgling galleries. They quickly spotted the new Galerie Schmidt, a two-storey square building with tall *faux*-Georgian windows, two on each floor framing a large entrance, over which the gallery's name was emblazoned in a fashionable lower-case typeface. They climbed a few steps up to enter the fray.

Johnny knew he was a bit pissed, but he didn't really care. It was rare these days that he let himself go like this, but he felt like he wanted to celebrate a little. The album was finished now and would soon be released. The tour was taking shape. Things were good for him. He had earned the right to celebrate. He picked up another glass of champagne and looked around. Mark had gone off to find Arthur, so he had some time on his own to take things in. The new space was starting to fill up now. It was a very different crowd to the opening in Paris – generally younger and scruffier. He recognised people from the Groucho but also from what he thought of as the 'Shoreditch crowd'. Many of the artists from *Sensation* seemed to be there. He had spotted and waved at Damien Hirst, the Chapman Brothers, Tracey Emin, Sarah Lucas and nodded at others that he knew less well but recognised, like Gavin Turk and Marc Quinn. Damien and Tracey in particular were quite well known now, even outside artistic circles They all seemed to support one another at these openings, which was good to see. The music world felt somehow more competitive and less authentic by comparison. An area in the middle of the large space was curtained off, he assumed for the unveiling of Arthur's new work. He had to admit that Caroline had done an amazing job on the space in a short time. Its gleaming white walls and high-tech lighting system were bang up to date and oozed understated minimalism. There were other artists exhibiting around the walls – mainly large abstract paintings – but Arthur's work was definitely the centrepiece curtained off in the centre of the room. His performance in Paris had created a buzz in London as well as Paris, so there was an air of expectancy in the room. His work was entitled *Personality Traits*, which gave little away.

'You look like you've had a few sherbets.' It was typical of Marty to say it like he saw it.

'As a matter of fact, I have, but I have managed to maintain control of my faculties until now. I'll let you know if I need assistance. Good evening, by the way, Marty.' His father did seem to have a knack for dampening the mood.

'Evening, son. Don't worry, I'll look out for you.'

There had been a lot of irony in what Johnny had said, but this had passed Marty by. At least his father was finally trying to take care of him.

'Thanks. So, what's your role in tonight's festivities?

'Well, I'm overseeing, just keeping an eye on things in case anything goes wrong.'

'What could go wrong then?'

'I can't tell you, I'm sworn to secrecy, but between you and me Arthur's trying something that he hasn't done before.'

'No surprises there then. How are you two getting on, by the way?'

'Pretty well, I'd say, but you'd have to ask Arthur.'

'I haven't seen him yet.'

'He's getting ready. I'm just off to give him a hand. Enjoy the show.'

At that moment Mark and Henri both appeared.

'Henri, you French twat.' Johnny greeted Henri with a bear hug. Henri gave him a thin smile when he released him.

'Good evening, my English chum.'

Johnny had the impression that Henri was a little out of sorts. 'You need some champagne, mate. You don't quite look your usual arrogant self.'

'Just feeling a little tired, *mon pote*. It's been a hectic few weeks.'

'I thought you looked a little under the weather, too, Henri,' Mark interjected. 'I didn't want to say anything, but Johnny doesn't like to hold back, as you know.'

'How's the beautiful Caroline, mate? You're punching well above your weight there.' No let up from Johnny.

'She is as beautiful as ever.'

The lights started to dim in the room.

'We need to get down to the front by the curtain. Marty tells me there's going to be a bit of a show.'

***

Mark followed Johnny and Henri towards the front of the crowd, which was starting to mill around in front of the surrounding curtain. His stomach was still tight with nerves. He really hoped that Arthur didn't make a fool of himself. Music began to play over the PA; Mark recognised it immediately as the introduction to 'Bela Lugosi's Dead' by Bauhaus. The swirling guitar began to fill the room with anticipation. The music faded before the vocals started, and a voice, which Mark immediately recognised as Marty's, started to speak. It was now almost dark. The curtains slowly drew back.

'Good evening, ladies and gentlemen. Welcome to the exhibition of Arthur Swale's continuing series of representations of personality disorders.'

As Marty was speaking, a spotlight powered up, illuminating

two figures dressed in black. One was Arthur and the other was Marty who was speaking through a small wireless microphone. Marty was holding something that Mark could not yet make out.

'You will all have seen the first of these artworks, the now famous *Narcissist*. Tonight, you will also be introduced to *The Obsessive Compulsive* and *The Paranoiac*, which stand behind us. But first, we offer a live representation of the fourth personality disorder, *The Histrionic*. For those of you who are not familiar with this personality type, these individuals need to be the centre of attention and love to entertain. It is with this in mind that our artist, Arthur Swale, will now escape from a straitjacket . . .' Marty paused for a moment then exclaimed in the style of a music hall compère '. . . before your very eyes!'

The announcement caused an intake of breath and a general hubbub in the crowd as Marty proceed to buckle Arthur into a straitjacket. Marty described what he was doing as he fitted the jacket. What the fuck are they up to? thought Mark. It appeared to be a real straitjacket, buckling at the back with the arms at the front.

'And now I'm buckling the back of the jacket as tightly as I can with the arms crossed at the front. This is a genuine straitjacket of the type used until relatively recently to secure the mentally ill.'

By now a mute Arthur was trussed up like a chicken. Marty turned Arthur around in a circle to demonstrate the security of the jacket, then he pushed Arthur away and shouted 'Go!' at the top of his voice. Arthur began to wriggle in the jacket, seeming to work his arms backwards and forwards. This carried on for a couple of minutes or so, with the crowd becoming quite animated, shouting words of encouragement. Suddenly Arthur appeared to have more freedom of movement and wrestled his right arm over his head giving him movement of both arms. This allowed him to manipulate the buckles behind him until he could open the back of the jacket and tear his arms out of the overlong sleeves. He twirled the jacket over his head to loud cheers, and the lights began to come up, illuminating *The Narcissist* in the centre behind Arthur with the other two new works on either side. There was a long round of applause for a grinning, crazy-haired Arthur as all three works were now completely illuminated behind him. He moved off to the side as the house lights gradually lit up the whole room once again. Mark was rather stupefied by what he had just seen, and it had him rooted to the spot. Arthur was in the middle of a crowd of well-wishers. He hadn't been joking about Houdini, had he? But was this really art? It was certainly entertainment, but Mark wasn't quite as convinced as he had been in Paris.

'Did you know about that? What a hoot,' Johnny chuckled as he approached.

'No, I didn't know about it. I'm a little perplexed to be honest. Was that art?'

'It was definitely Arthur behaving like Arthur. If that's art, then it was art. Who cares, really. I thought it was good fun. He's such a fucking twat. I'm going to go and tell him that, too.'

Johnny strode over to the group of people around Arthur, and Mark heard him telling him what a fucking twat he was in a loud voice. The group laughed along with the joke. Johnny was good in the limelight, especially after a few drinks. Mark took the opportunity to take a look at the two new exhibits. He was immediately drawn to the piece to the left of *The Narcissist*. This was labelled *The Obsessive Compulsive*, and Mark could see why. It was the upper half of a male human body, modelled a little like a shop mannequin, with its blank face and wig of brown hair. The figure was slightly bent over a sink that had water running into it from a tap, scrubbing at his hands with a brush. The speed of the movement was the disturbing element, as the model was working at fast-forward speed. The sequence lasted a couple of minutes, after which the model stopped, straightened its back, brought its hands up to its eyes then, as if its hands were not yet clean enough, resumed scrubbing for another two minutes. This whole process then repeated on a loop. Mark was slightly mesmerised by it and watched the model repeat the process, like a robot but somehow more human than that. He managed to pull himself away from this figure to inspect the one on the right, titled *The Paranoiac.* This was another mannequin-style figure, but this time clothed in a black hoodie, with the hood pulled over its head. The facial features of this piece were dark, and its brow was furrowed. Most of the time its gaze was looking downwards, but every minute or so it took a furtive look over its shoulder. Again, Mark felt quite drawn into the piece and stood watching it for a while, waiting for the furtive looks to appear. His mildly hypnotic state was disturbed by an announcement over the PA. He looked around and saw Caroline Schmidt with a microphone. She started to make a speech. She was an accomplished speaker, Mark had to admit, oozing understated wealth in her black dress and discreet but highly valuable jewellery. She had a slight accent in English, but it was hard to place, a smattering of French intonation and a little mid-Atlantic pronunciation. Mark found her a little cold but quite enjoyed how she managed to appear to out-confidence even Henri, whom Mark considered an enviably confident individual. She was evidently making an announcement, so Mark tuned in.

'And so, we are delighted to formally announce this evening that Arthur Swale will be the British Council's UK representative at the Venice Biennale in 1999. You will be able to visit Venice to see the exhibits from April next year, a few short months away.'

So, what could they expect for the Biennale, Mark wondered. It seemed like Arthur could not put a foot wrong right now, but Mark's natural inclination made him nervous on Arthur's behalf. On the theme of the last exhibition, pride comes before a fall, and Mark hoped that Arthur was not heading for one. He felt as if there was an inverse relationship between Arthur's fame and their own closeness: as Arthur's fame grew, Mark felt the distance between them widening.

VENICE

APRIL 1999

Henri made his way to the back of the boat and watched as the skipper of their water taxi offered a hand to Caroline to help her onboard. Henri had become used to the attention that men paid his girlfriend wherever they went. At the beginning of their relationship this had bothered him, but now, strangely, he felt more at ease. The jealousy had waned, he realised, once their physical relationship had taken its turn towards sado-masochism. It was his guilty secret; his beautiful partner humiliated him in the bedroom, and he acquiesced. From the start she had always been dominant sexually, but when the slaps across the face had started he had been too shocked to complain, partly because he could see that it turned her on. She had then asked to tie him up, and again he had agreed. The result of his compliance had led to what he now understood to be an abusive physical relationship. Outside the bedroom nothing about this was mentioned; it was as if nothing had changed. However, the humiliation in the bedroom had created an obstacle for Henri; he felt he would never feel really close to Caroline while he felt degraded by what they did together. The irony of the guilty secret was that all other areas of his life, particularly his business life, had flourished since they had reconnected. At the bank his career went from strength to strength as the introductions Caroline made for him bore fruit, producing banking relationships with wealthy investors in the art world and beyond. He continued to share financially in the benefits of Arthur Swale's increased fame, as well as through a couple of other up-and-coming artists he had introduced to Caroline through his own ever-increasing connections in the art world. He and Caroline continued to travel widely beyond Paris and Geneva, to London, New York, even Hong Kong. They had begun to appear occasionally in the gossip columns of newspapers in London and Paris, as the contemporary art market continued to take a global hold on public interest.

As the water taxi moved away from the dock at Venice airport, Henri put his arm around Caroline's shoulders. It was warm for April, and they sat at the back of the boat out in the open, enjoying the late-afternoon sunshine. The boat chugged slowly out into the lagoon, following the speed restrictions, before its nose suddenly emerged from the waves as their pilot accelerated into the open water further out and pointed them in the direction of the ancient buildings and canals of Venice. The combination of the soft, warm sunlight and salty breeze heightened Henri's senses. He put his guilty secret to the back of his mind and smiled at Caroline; she returned his smile and gripped his hand tightly.

'I wonder what surprises our English friend has for us tomorrow?' Caroline was obviously a little anxious about the opening of Arthur's exhibition.

'Well, we've already seen the art, so there is nothing to shock us there. I'm guessing it's his "introductory performance" that's bothering you.'

'He's refused to tell anyone what it involves. The only thing I know is that he has asked the Biennale management to ensure that there is an ambulance on site.'

'Really? That sounds a little extreme.' Henri smiled. Arthur could be relied upon to cause trouble.

'It's no joke, Henri. I hope he's not going to do anything stupid.'

'I hope he *does* do something stupid; that's how we get all the publicity.'

Caroline punched him playfully on the arm, laughing, 'I guess you're right. All publicity is good publicity?'

'Something like that.'

Within a few quick minutes they were approaching the main island of Venice; its quintessential collection of domes, towers and ancient roofs rising above the water and gradually homing into view. To Henri there were few sights more alluring than arriving in Venice by boat. Whatever his mood, whatever the situation, he was always excited by this journey across the famous lagoon. As a small boat they were able to avoid the northerly entrance to the Grand Canal and turn to the south between the island of Murano and the eastern side of the main island and its historic centre, past the Madonna dell'Orto to their right, entering the system of canals almost furtively through the back door, as they turned into Canale della Misericordia. They were staying at the Hotel Ca'Sagredo on the Grand Canal itself, but their short cut first took them down the narrower watery passageways and past the smaller, less-exclusive buildings of Cannaregio; these were less ostentatious but equally striking to the eye, as the sun reflected off their pink, ochre and pale-blue walls. Without warning, at the end of the narrow canal by which they had entered, the towering palazzi of the Grand Canal itself were suddenly upon them. The wide expanse of water was much more like the open lagoon, full of rocking boats of various sizes, from vaporetti, barges, and gondolas to rowing boats. Their own chic wooden motor launch, suddenly dwarfed in the traffic, turned sharp left, and very soon they were tying up at the mooring of their hotel, just a little north of the Rialto Bridge and slap bang in the middle of the most beautiful city in the world.

As the hotel staff took the bags off their boat Henri felt a sudden urge to take a moment to contemplate the view, smoke a cigarette and bask in the fading sun. He turned to Caroline.

'Do you mind? I'm just going to have a quick drink and a cigarette on my favourite terrace.'

'Of course not, *chéri*. Take a breath. I have calls to make in any case.'

Henri quickly found a seat on the terrace at the front of the hotel next to the mooring looking out on to the water and across it to the famous Rialto market. He had thought he was pretty energetic before he met Caroline, but life with her was lived at a constantly fast pace. He enjoyed taking a moment from time to time over a coffee or a beer, just to gather his thoughts and plan his moves. He ordered a negroni, lit a Disque Bleu and looked out at the organised chaos floating on the water in front of him. Vessels small and large moved in both directions, swerving to miss one another as necessary; there were commercial barges carrying all sorts of produce from building material to groceries, gondolas with cargoes of Japanese tourists, water taxis, water buses and then simply local Venetians going about their business in their little speedboats. All of these modes of water transport bobbed and weaved their way up and down in front of him. Somehow he found this chaos meditative. He reflected on the coming evening's events. Tonight there was a drinks reception where he would be glad-handing the great and the good of the Biennale, followed by dinner with the old crew. He had managed to talk Caroline, for once, into side-stepping dinner with business people and getting together with the original poker school of Johnny, Mark and Sophie. He hadn't seen any of them since the Galerie Schmidt opening in London the previous year. Caroline had arranged for them all to stay at the same hotel, so they must either be here already or arriving shortly. He was looking forward to seeing all of them, but he realised that it was Sophie in particular that he had missed. It was only very recently that he had thought back on their relationship; he recognised that he had probably behaved badly when it had petered to a close. He had Caroline in his sights by then and had become single-minded in his pursuit of her; this had inevitably led to the end of anything that had been left between Sophie and him. She had been a wounded soul when the relationship had begun, wounded by Johnny's fecklessness and the humiliation of the incident with Mark. He admitted to himself that he had taken advantage of the situation, but why not? She was a beautiful woman in need of some tenderness. He had certainly provided that, and he hoped she remembered that he had.

'Fancy meeting a bloke like you in a place like this.' Henri felt a hand on his shoulder and the dulcet tones of his old friend Johnny. Right on cue, but the wrong partner in the couple. He got up and gave his old friend a hug.

As they sat down, he hailed a waiter over.

'Johnny, you have to join me in a negroni. The Venetians love their spritzes, but I prefer the full weight of a negroni. It's ideally suited to a man of your discerning taste and capacity for alcohol.'

'Enlighten me, Henri.'

Johnny still wore his fair hair quite long, and it framed his lean, freckled features. He was wearing round Lennon-style sunglasses, which prevented Henri from seeing his eyes, but he knew that they would be a little red around the edges. Johnny seemed to be on rather than off the booze. There was no real middle ground with him.

'Well, so the story goes, in a bar in Florence, towards the beginning of this century, a Count Negroni decided to try gin in his Americano instead of soda, and the negroni was born. So, equal parts gin, Campari and red vermouth, stirred and poured over ice, accompanied by a slice of orange. What better way could there be to complement the view?'

'Sold, my friend.'

Johnny had already lit a Marlboro Light, on which he was feverishly puffing. Henri suspected he might be back on the coke, too. He seemed a little wired.

'Are you OK, man. You seem a little jumpy.'

'Nice of you to ask, Henri.' He had known Johnny long enough to understand his breed of sarcasm. 'I'm a bit strung out, to be honest. I've literally just jumped off the tour bus to be here for a couple of days. I promised Sophie I'd come. We played in Milan last night, then I took a train down this morning. I seem to have gone back to propping myself up with a little snort here and there. Nothing too serious. Don't mention it to Sophie, will you?'

'Sure. No problem. Where is Sophie by the way?' At least Johnny wasn't hiding his drug use. That was encouraging. Well, only from Sophie anyway.

'She's coming via Paris. She's arriving by train with Juste and Véronique.'

'Of course. I'd forgotten. I think they told me.'

'They're due in shortly, I think. She's thick as thieves with those two now.' Johnny's drink arrived, and he took a large slug of it. 'Fuck me, Henri, that's brutal, mate.'

'You're supposed to sip it. *À petites, mon brave.*'

Johnny took another smaller sip. 'Just the job, mate, just the job,' he said smiling. Henri realised how nice it was to be alone with his old friend, the perpetually slightly wired rockstar Johnny Jones. 'You know, if I didn't know better, I'd think there was something going on between Sophie and those two,' Johnny continued.

'What do you mean?'

'Well, exactly that. Particularly Juste. They seem very tight, she and Sophie. I don't think Sophie likes girls, though, you know, sexually.'

'I would imagine not. I don't think you need to worry.' Henri knew how predatory Juste could be, and he was sure Johnny probably did need to worry. He changed the subject. 'So, I think we're having dinner near the hotel tonight. Mark should be here too, Sophie, the girls, Caroline and I think that's it.'

'No Arthur and Marty?'

'I did ask Caroline, but apparently they're busy getting everything ready. We won't see them until the opening tomorrow.'

'They seem to have become very close. I don't hear much from Marty these days. He seemed actually to want to be my father for a little while.'

'Well, at least you'll see him tomorrow.'

'How's the blonde bombshell?'

'Caroline? Unstoppable.'

'I don't doubt it!'

They both inhaled on their cigarettes and looked wistfully out over the canal.

***

It was the first time today that Mark had stopped rushing. He had rushed to work in London this morning to pack in what he needed to do before the short trip to Venice. The last meeting had dragged, which, in turn, had made him late for his plane, so he had taken one of the new motorcycle taxis out to Heathrow, ensuring he arrived at the airport with just over an hour to go. He had been cutting it fine to make it to the dinner tonight, but fortunately the plane had been on time, the vaporetto from the airport had been on time and now here he was ensconced in Vini da Gigio a couple of minutes from the hotel, in a picturesque spot, looking out over a beautiful little canal lined by pastel-coloured Renaissance buildings. He was sitting between Sophie and Johnny, watching Henri order Venetian specialities for the table. Juste, however, was refusing to let Henri have it all his own way. The discussion was in a mixture of Italian, French and English. Mark sat back and watched, a little in awe of the multilingual debate.

'If we're having *cicchetti* first, then we have to have a Venetian white wine, not a Prosecco.' Juste was insistent on this point.

'What are *cicchetti*?' Mark asked Sophie in a whisper. He was hoping to bury the hatchet for good on this trip.

'I think they're like a Venetian appetiser, little things on toasted bread, that kind of thing,' she whispered back.

'However, I agree with you on the next course, we have to have *sardele in saor* for one of our starters.' Juste had finally agreed with one of Henri's choices.

'For the uninitiated, that's fried sardine with *saor*, which is a kind of Venetian sweet-and-sour sauce.' Henri was trying to include everyone in his choices. Mark would just accept what was ordered. Only a short time ago the idea of eating things on spec would have filled him with anxiety; it was a good thing that Arthur had educated him in broadening his palate. The debate continued through the courses. Mark had noticed that the waiter, resplendent in a waist-to-floor apron, seemed to relish his customers' enthusiasm for their choices, interjecting where he felt they should be steered towards a particular dish or wine.

'So, if we are having *seppie alla Veneziana con polenta*, will you let me go to Barolo for the red wine?'

'A fine choice,' said Juste. The waiter joined in the enthusiastic agreement. Mark was a little lost at this point; he had no idea what had been ordered as a main course, but at least it seemed like they'd finished ordering.

Their group of seven was seated in a small wood-panelled area of the restaurant, giving an intimate feel to the dinner. Sophie was to Mark's left at the head of the table, with Johnny to his right and Véronique opposite. Caroline, Juste and Henri were at the other end, but the table was small enough for everyone to feel that they were part of the group.

'So, what can we expect tomorrow?' Sophie asked Mark. He noticed that there was no undercurrent in her tone. Maybe the passing of some more time actually had healed the old wounds.

'Well, to be honest, I haven't seen a lot of Arthur for the last few weeks. I don't generally get invited to the studio while he's working on a project, and then he's been over here for a couple of weeks with Marty getting everything ready for the big day.'

'But don't you have an idea of what he's going to do?'

'Well, I do know that the exhibition is the final version of the personality disorders. I think there's ten of them. You weren't at the last one in London, but, as Johnny probably would have told you, what Arthur did was perform *The Histrionic* disorder. My guess would be that he might do that again to open the exhibition. That's my main worry anyway.' He laughed nervously.

They had small plates of *cicchetti* put in front of then, and their glasses were filled with a Venetian white wine. Mark bit into a piece of toasted bread topped with a creamy white coloured mixture.

'That's delicious, but I've no idea what it is.'

'*Baccalà*,' said Véronique opposite grinning. She obviously understood more than she let on.

'That's salt cod, I think,' said Sophie.

The wine, too, Mark found to be deliciously dry with an appley tartness, a perfect accompaniment. He was turning into a proper foodie.

'So, you're fairly sure we can expect another performance tomorrow morning?'

'I think so. I don't suppose it will be a repeat of the straitjacket, though. I reckon it will be something else. He hasn't told me what, but he drops things in now and then. Houdini has been mentioned in passing.'

'Shit. That's taking it to another level. Are we expecting water tanks and padlocks then?' Sophie couldn't help herself.

'I hope not,' said Mark nervously.

'You know, I'm pleased for you that you've met Arthur. You seem very happy.'

'Thank you. I really am. It's very big of you to say so. I'm sorry for what happened between Johnny and me. I hope we can put it behind us.'

'You know, it will always be there, but I feel like we need to move on, so yes, let's try to put it behind us.'

Mark felt a lump in his throat. It was big of Sophie to be like this;

he wondered what had caused the change of heart. Maybe it was just the passing of time, but he appreciated it.

***

Juste decided that everyone should change places just as the main course was arriving. Sophie was allowed to remain where she was at the head of the table; she felt a flutter of excitement when Juste positioned herself to her left, changing places with Véronique. Now to her right sat Caroline, whom she didn't actually know that well.

'I thought you might need a break from that pig who sucked your husband's cock,' said Juste in French and in a loudish stage whisper. Juste knew Mark wouldn't understand the remark and gave out a loud cackle. Sophie noticed Caroline raising her eyebrows, having obviously heard and understood what Juste had said. She imagined Caroline was not privy to the details of the incident Juste was referring to, unless Henri had told her, of course, but that seemed pretty unlikely.

'We have made our peace,' said Sophie again in French. It seemed like they would be speaking in French while the boys spoke English at the other end of the table. Caroline was too discreet to ask for any more information.

'*Putain*. Really? You are worth more than that, *ma chérie*.'

'Forgive others not because they deserve forgiveness but because you deserve peace. I can't remember where I heard that, but I'm beginning to understand its sentiment.'

'That's admirable,' said Caroline. 'I'm not sure that it's a life lesson I've learned yet.'

'Me neither,' said Juste, letting out another loud cackle. 'You deserve better anyway,' she said to Sophie, touching her face gently as she did so.

The gesture was just a bit too familiar, and Sophie felt herself colouring a little. Fortunately the cuttlefish was arriving, and a plateful of this black, inky dish was placed in front of each of them, diverting their attention from her pink face. Sophie and Juste met infrequently, but the frisson she felt when Juste touched her remained. The night they had spent together in Brede last year remained their only one together, and Sophie thought of it often.

'Wow, that is absolutely delicious,' Caroline said, perhaps keen to change the subject. Sophie bit into a piece of cuttlefish coated in an unctuous, dark-blue, almost black sauce. It had a rich, deep, earthy but fishy flavour that perfectly complemented the soft, tender, perfectly cooked mollusc.

'You're right, that is fabulous,' said Sophie. 'Great choice, Henri,' she called up the table.

'Yes, a great choice, darling,' Caroline joined her in congratulating Henri. He raised a glass of Barolo to them from the far end of the table. Sophie wondered if Caroline knew about her past with Henri. Again, she doubted if he had told her, as there was no real upside in conveying the information. Henri rarely did anything without a motive.

'So, do you have a better idea of what we can expect tomorrow, Caroline? I was asking Mark earlier, but he didn't seem to know any details.'

'Well, it's quite hush-hush, but there's no harm in you knowing the night before, I don't suppose. Even I don't know everything. Arthur always likes to keep things up his sleeve. That said, what I am expecting is an exhibition of the completed ten personality disorder pieces, with nine sculptures and one performance piece. The performance piece will open the exhibition, and it will take place outside the British Pavilion. Arthur will perform the piece, but that is all I know. Even the British Council haven't been told exactly what he's going to do.'

'You have no clues?'

'The only clue I have is that he has told the organisers that he has arranged for an ambulance to be on site during the performance.'

'Really?'

'Yes, really.'

***

Henri sat back in the comfortable sofa in the bar at the hotel and took a moment to take in his group of friends. He had his arm proprietorially around Caroline, who was next to him resting her head on his shoulder; she was not normally a night owl. To his right Johnny and Mark were deep in conversation on a couple of armchairs. Sat opposite were Sophie, Juste and Véronique; they were rather squashed together on a sofa designed for two, and this was causing a great deal of merriment. Juste in particular, squeezed in the middle between the others, looked very much at home. Now that Johnny had mentioned some kind of connection between Juste and Sophie, it had begun to look obvious to Henri. Juste's hand rested casually on Sophie's thigh; it could have been interpreted as a friendly gesture, but Henri knew Juste better than that. Sophie was doing nothing to demonstrate that she felt uncomfortable and everything to suggest that she was enjoying the physical closeness. Henri wondered if they were lovers. Almost certainly they were.

'You know, I think I'm going to go up to bed. We have a big day tomorrow. Come up soon, darling.' Caroline said her goodbyes, and Henri watched as she walked out of the bar into the vast reception area with its high, beamed, palazzo ceilings. Despite their dark secrets he still found her very attractive, and his eyes lingered on her as she sashayed away. Now he had the chance to speak to Sophie. He needed to shift the nagging feeling of humiliation he felt stemming from his compliance with Caroline's sadism. He could see that Sophie was a little drunk but not so drunk that she couldn't offer him a sympathetic ear. He leaned across the spritz-laden table between them. The three women were speaking in French; he chose to interrupt her in English. Somehow it seemed more polite.

'Excuse me, Sophie, there's something that Caroline wanted me to ask you. Can I have a quick word at the bar?'

'Sure.' Sophie made no fuss and walked straight over to the bar with her unfinished spritz in hand. Henri followed her with the Armagnac that he had been nursing. They left Juste and Véronique in a physical and verbal tussle on the sofa.

'I hope you don't mind, Sophie, we don't get much of a chance to talk these days.'

'Since you left me hanging in Paris last year, you mean?' Sophie was smiling as she said this, which Henri interpreted as a thawing in hostilities.

'I know. I'm sorry for the way things ended between us.'

'Thank you for apologising, Henri. I know you don't really mean it, but thank you. Something better came along. I can see that. And she was single, she wasn't married to one of your best friends and, most of all, she was very beautiful and very connected.' Sophie was now laughing as she said all this. 'The truth of it is that things were pretty much over between us anyway.' She had stopped laughing now. 'I realise that now. It was for the best, just a little hurtful at the time.'

'Talking about old times . . . ?' Johnny had suddenly appeared from nowhere. 'Just kidding,' he said putting his arms around them both. 'I'm not interrupting, just on the way to the bog.' With that he tottered off.

'Just a little reminder that, while he may not be that bothered about what we did, he doesn't condone it.' Sophie was back to smiling again.

'Well, we both know how he let you down in the past, too, and you seem to have put that behind you.'

'Forgive and forget – or, at least, try to forget.' She laughed again. She looked good when she laughed, her full lips parted. She was wearing her dark-brown hair a little longer, and Henri thought it suited her.

'Do you remember that time in Paris when you asked for my advice, at Le Meurice?'

'How could I forget?'

'Well, now I have something a little embarrassing that I want your advice about.'

'You, Henri, embarrassed? That is a first.'

'It's quite delicate. It concerns Caroline and I.'

'You've come to the wrong person for romantic advice.'

'It's more sexual advice.'

'I'm not sure I'm qualified in that area either.'

'She hits me.' He blurted it out, but quietly.

'What do you mean?'

'When we're having sex, she hits me, slaps me hard around the face. And I can't stop her. I just comply. I let her do it.' Although he was embarrassed, Henri immediately felt a little better now that he had told someone.

'Well, you won't be the first to indulge in a little S&M, Henri. Whatever floats your boat. It's not my thing, but I thought you were broadminded?'

'I suppose I am, but this is humiliating, and yet I still let it happen.' He said this in French for emphasis.

'Do you mean that your male pride is affected because a woman is hitting you? You wouldn't feel humiliated if it was the other way around, would you? Why don't you stop her if you don't like it?'

'I'm not sure. Once I let her do it the first couple of times, it became difficult to say no.'

'I think you might secretly like it, Henri.' Sophie began to laugh again. 'Maybe she's found your weakness. I never did, neither at the poker table nor in the bedroom, but maybe she has.'

'So what can I do about it?'

'I think you need to decide whether or not you like it before you do anything else. If you don't want it to happen but it continues, then it's probably abusive. If, deep down, you like it, then there's not really a problem. One way or another, you just need to man up, Henri!' Now Sophie was laughing again. Henri was laughing, too, but he hadn't found what she had said very funny.

***

Momentarily Sophie wondered if she had been too hard on Henri. But it was a short-lived fear; she realised that she was in fact quite pleased that he had finally exposed a chink in his armour. It was also predictably chauvinistic to feel humiliated by Caroline roughing him up a little. Caroline was never going to be her best friend, but it amused her to think of her taking charge of such a confident man. He was clearly troubled by the situation, but Sophie knew that this was a wobble rather than a serious problem; it was good for a man like Henri, attractive and charming as he was, to be emotionally tested. It might even help him to develop his empathy gene.

'OK, baby, it's time for us to spend some quality time together.' Johnny had reappeared. Sophie knew what quality time meant. She took a furtive look over to their table and saw Juste and Véronique still involved in one of their minor spats. Mark was nowhere to be found. Her options seemed to be joining an argument with the girls or drunk sex with her long-lost husband. What would her new fantasy spiritual guide Tracey Emin choose? She was fairly sure she would go for the drunk sex, so drunk sex it was to be, provided Johnny managed to stay awake. He actually seemed quite perky, so it might be quite fun; she might even use some of the techniques that Henri had just described.

***

Johnny sat in the back of the water taxi feeling slightly queasy as they bumped up and down on the waters of the Grand Canal. He had snorted a furtive line of coke to kickstart his day, and, while it had lifted his mood, he really needed a drink to improve his overall wellbeing. The smell of Venice filled his nostrils, a combination of seawater and drains, which seemed ever present. Sophie was to his left, chatting animatedly in French with Juste and Véronique, pointing at the glorious lines of palazzi on either side of them rising in the morning light, all three of them buzzing at the prospect of the opening of the exhibition later that morning. He and Sophie had managed to speak to Amy a little earlier before she left for school. She was staying with Sophie's parents in Rye, and now that they had a mobile phone it was much easier to stay in touch. That conversation with their daughter, and the fact that they had made love the previous night with some gusto, helped him feel both emotionally and physically closer to Sophie. He knew that the long weeks he was away on tour were not helpful to their relationship. He also knew that he tended to lapse into substance abuse as a crutch to get him through these periods. He found that the highs of touring were very high and the lows very low; the highs at the concerts were like nothing else he had ever experienced. Now that he was the lead singer as well as the guitarist in his own band the adulation both from the original Swerve fanbase, as well as a growing crowd of new fans, was almost too much. At the end of each performance, he was bursting with adrenaline, and he found he could only calm himself by hitting the booze pretty hard straight after the performance. 'Dead Dad' was quite a big hit now, having charted as high as number eight in the UK charts and made the top ten in other charts across Europe. He was quite a big star now in Sweden and Denmark, although the needle had not really moved in the USA. They seemed less inspired by the whole Britpop vibe. Johnny had never thought of himself as a Britpop act; his first brush with fame with Swerve had predated Britpop, and he now felt that the movement was on the wane. There was definitely something going on with big beat and the whole dance scene, however, and he was really pleased with how the new songs were going down; people seemed to love the big beat influence. He took

Sophie's hand, and she squeezed his as he did so. In the moment he felt like there was a connection between them that they sometimes lost. He rallied at this thought and decided to drag himself into the day ahead.

'Come on, girls, my French isn't good enough to keep up with you lot.'

'Ah, Monsieur le Rockstar, you are still alive. I had thought your hangover might be terminal.' Juste, easily switching from French to English, seemed to be on top form as ever, despite the previous night's festivities.

'It's nothing a glass of champagne won't sort out, my dear.' Sophie squeezed his hand again. She seemed to be on his side today.

They were approaching the end of the Grand Canal, one of the busiest areas of any waterway in the Floating City. There was an immediate increase in the swell of the water as they rounded the southernmost point of San Marco and entered the larger Canale della Giudecca, which, in turn, became the open lagoon itself. Véronique pointed excitedly to the Doge's Palace and a glimpse of St Mark's Square on their left as they bumped along the waves towards their destination at Arsenale. Their skipper moved towards the shore and slowed the boat to walking place before tying up at the mooring at Giardini, a stone's throw from the Biennale.

As they disembarked and walked up through the gardens Juste turned to Sophie and Johnny. 'Ask me anything you like, by the way. I can guide you around. I have been to the Biennale before,' she said.

Of course she has, thought Johnny. Sophie caught his eye and smiled.

'Where do I get a glass of champagne?' He asked, partly in jest and partly out of necessity.

'I'm sure the *rosbifs* will have plenty to drink at their pavilion. It's actually a very pretty building, as I remember.'

'I read that it's a bit like an Italian country house.'

'Not a bad description,' said Juste. Véronique was making faces behind Juste's back for Sophie and Johnny. She knew that Juste was being slightly pompous, even if she hadn't completely understood the conversation. Johnny liked Véronique; she was fun loving as well as elegant in an effortlessly French way. She carried her looks easily, and while she was a little overshadowed by Juste, she was no pushover.

They presented their invitations at the entrance, and there they were directed to the British Pavilion through a garden dotted with permanent exhibition buildings of huge variety, from what appeared to be repurposed Renaissance dock buildings through several centuries to others in a whole mishmash of twentieth-century architectural styles, each with the name of the country they represented on the front. Quite quickly they found themselves in front of the Palladian looking British Pavilion. The building itself was somewhat obscured by a collection of people, crates, a small crane, various other vehicles and what looked like an ambulance crew, resplendent in hi-vis orange uniforms. There was something about the way an Italian wore a uniform; the word 'peacocking' came to Johnny. He assumed that the ambulance itself must be a boat, as there really were no roads. He looked across the park to the moorings in the lagoon and, sure enough, there was a Venetian water ambulance with one of the crew lounging next to it.

'So, what now?' said Sophie.

Yes, what now? he thought to himself.

***

Mark had arrived early at the Biennale site by vaporetto. He had woken up at sunrise feeling apprehensive about the day ahead. He still hadn't seen Arthur and knew he wouldn't until he got himself to the venue at Arsenale, so he had decided to get down there nice and early. The splendour of the boat trip down the Grand Canal had been a little lost on him, as he had spent the time trying to manage his nerves. He had a bad feeling about the show; he couldn't quite place why, but he felt anxious. He had found his way to the exhibition park, a short walk from the vaporetto stop, and asked for directions to the British Pavilion. And now here he was, stood in front of a glass tank that was probably ten feet high, filled about a third of the way up with a sandy-looking soil. This did not help his anxiety. There were various people milling around, one of whom was Marty. He quickly made his way over to him.

'Marty,' he called.

'Blimey, you're early, Mark. You know we don't start for another two or three hours.'

'Yes, I'm aware of that, Marty. Where's Arthur? I wish he would carry a mobile, then at least I could talk to him to find out what's going on. He didn't want me to come down here last night, which is why I'm down here early. What is going on? What is that glass tank for?'

'I'm sorry, mate, I'm sworn to secrecy. You're best off speaking to the main man.'

'Well, where is he?'

'I'm not actually sure. The last time I saw him was at breakfast. He told me he was going to go and prepare himself mentally for the day ahead, then he scarpered. I haven't seen him since then.'

Mark looked at his watch. It was 9 a.m. 'What time was that?'

'About an hour ago, I suppose.'

'What time is the exhibition opening?'

'I was told that the performance will be at 11.30.'

'So, there is going to be a performance?'

'As I said, Mark, my lips are sealed.' Marty could be a very irritating man.

'Have you any idea where he is?'

'No. You know what he's like. He does what the fuck he wants. He could be anywhere.'

'Right, well I suppose I'll just go and get a coffee then.'

'Probably best.' Marty turned on his heels and moved towards a group of workers collected in front of a crane and a digger. The area around them looked more like a building site than an exhibition. Arthur could be such a massive pain the arse, but there was nothing for it other than to wait it out.

***

Henri shook hands with yet another member of the British Council party and did his best to remain charming, for Caroline's sake. These people were, after all, the people who had chosen Arthur to represent his country, and Henri hoped that the publicity would continue to raise Arthur's profile. It would also raise Caroline's profile, and, again, that could only accumulate credit for him. He felt a tap on his shoulder and turned around to see Mark standing behind him looking a little agitated. He happily excused himself from the meet and greet to see what Mark wanted.

'Have you seen Arthur?' The lack of a greeting confirmed, as Henri suspected, that Mark was a little distressed.

'Good morning, Mark. No, I haven't seen Arthur yet. I imagine he is preparing for the performance.

'So, you know about it? Marty won't tell me a thing, and Arthur's gone missing.'

'Well, I don't know much, but I do know that he's going to do another performance of *The Histrionic*. I'm guessing the big glass tank full of soil is a bit of a giveaway. *Calme-toi*, Mark. It's just Arthur being Arthur. He's the living embodiment of histrionic. None of this should be surprising you.'

'I know you're right. He is very unpredictable, and he does love to show off in public, but I have a bad feeling about this. Works of art don't normally need to be supervised by an ambulance crew.'

'Well, it's coming up to 11.30, *mon ami*. We shall know soon enough.'

'Are you sure you don't know any more than that?'

'My apologies, but I really don't. Neither does Caroline.'

'I'm going to check with Johnny and Sophie. That man is going to get a serious bollocking next time I see him for putting me through this.'

Mark turned on his heel to seek out the others. Henri was pretty sure that Arthur would not be getting what Mark referred to as a 'bollocking'. He was not a man to chastise. It was clear, however, that Mark was very nervous. He and Caroline had not thought to insist on knowing more about Arthur's performance; it was just part of the art. They had told the British Council that the fact there was an ambulance crew on site was just all part of the show, it was for effect, but they didn't really know that this was the case. Henri was sure that everything would be fine, that the ambulance crew really was for effect, and in an hour or so they would be feting Arthur once again for his performance.

***

Sophie was having a lovely time. They had managed to grab glasses of Prosecco from a passing waiter, and the last of her hangover had dissipated as the bubbles did their job. She felt like she had reconnected with Johnny last night without compromising the excitement she got from being around Juste. She was happy to be with people she loved, enjoying the excitement of a big event.

'Well, this should be fun,' she said. 'I wonder what he's going to do.'

'Something quite stupid,' Juste said in French.

'When we were in London, as you know, he escaped from a straitjacket. I should imagine that we're in for some more escapology,' said Johnny, ignoring Juste. 'I think it'll be fun. I had a quick chat with Marty, but he gave me nothing, so it's still a bit of a mystery.'

'At least Arthur is actually here now. I just had a quick chat with him. He's ready for the performance, but he still won't tell me what it is.' Sophie thought Mark seemed calmer now that he knew Arthur was no longer missing.

The PA system started crackling. They were stood on the steps in front of the Pavilion overlooking the large glass tank. There was a crowd of maybe a hundred or so, including what Sophie recognised as a group of journalists and photographers, milling around together towards the front. To Sophie they looked more like the British tabloid type of journalist than art critics. They certainly didn't look Italian; they were too scruffy in their cargo pants and baggy jackets for that to be the case. Marty appeared from stage left, dressed from head to toe in black, and grabbed the microphone from its stand.

'Good morning, ladies and gentlemen. *Buongiorno, signore e signori*. Arthur has asked me to introduce the opening performance of his Biennale show. You may have been wondering what a glass tank full of dirt is doing at an art exhibition. How can that be art? Well, Arthur believes that Houdini was the greatest performance artist of the modern age. He also believes that Houdini was a histrionic personality type, his epic performances encapsulating his extreme desire to be noticed by the world. What better way to celebrate the opening of an exhibition that is a homage to the ten personality disorders than to perform a tribute to one of the greatest histrionics of them all?' A buzz went around the small crowd at this point. 'Today, in Venice, in the Biennale Gardens,' by now Marty was almost shouting, 'Arthur Swale will be buried alive – and live to tell the tale.'

The hubbub in the crowd had now turned into an audible gasp.

Arthur appeared from behind the group of ambulance workers dressed from head to toe in black like Marty; he performed a theatrical bow to the crowd by way of introduction. In return, he received a hearty round of applause. Nervous encouragement, thought Sophie, clapping along. Next, a clear plastic or glass coffin-shaped box was wheeled on by two more helpers. They took the box off the trolley, put it on the ground and removed the lid. Arthur then stepped into the coffin and lay down. The two helpers replaced the lid, and Marty came forward with an armful of leather straps. With the assistance of the helpers, he fastened these around the coffin so that it was secure. Arthur lay inside motionless.

'Oh my God. What is he doing? We should get him to stop.' Mark was standing next to Sophie now, watching the proceedings, horrified at the prospect of what Arthur was about to do.

'He'll be fine,' Sophie heard Johnny say. 'I'm sure it's all under control, or he wouldn't be doing it.

'*Mais, c'est un fou.*' Juste had her hand over her mouth, as, almost before they knew it the coffin was lowered into the glass tank full of soil by a small crane, and a large digger came forward and began to pour more soil into the glass tank. In less than a minute the tank had been filled to a level of around six feet, and Arthur and the glass coffin had completely disappeared. Sophie felt nauseous, fear rising in the pit of her stomach. She knew that there must be a way out of this for Arthur and tried to reassure herself that he would have rehearsed this many times, but he really had actually just been buried alive. The crowd had gone strangely quiet. Marty stood silently in front of the coffin, looking at his watch in a slightly theatrical manner. Sophie guessed that when they had practised the performance, they had worked out the time that it took for Arthur to escape; if he hadn't appeared after that time had elapsed, then presumably there would be some kind of procedure to rescue him. She wondered how long it would be. How long could Arthur hold his breathe for? Or was it possible to breathe under that soil in the glass coffin? Like Johnny, her inclination was to assume that there was a technique to be used here, and that Arthur and Marty had control of the situation. However, the reality was inescapable. Arthur was at least three feet under, strapped into a coffin with no obvious means of escape.

Even if he did get out of the coffin, how would he tunnel his way through the soil without being able to breathe? The more she thought about it, the less she liked it.

'We need to stop this Sophie and go in and get Arthur out.' Mark was visibly panicking now.

At least a minute had gone by, and the nervous crowd were starting to vocalise their concern. Marty was still stood at the front looking at his watch, his body language somehow less confident about the situation than it had been.

Mark had clearly had enough. 'Come on, Johnny,' he said. 'We're getting him out.'

He started to push his way through the crowd on the steps, and Johnny followed. They were well into the second minute now. Sophie scanned the soil for any movement, and suddenly there was something, a small tremor on the surface of the soil. An encouraging noise went up from the crowd. Marty continued to look at his watch. By now Mark and Johnny had reached Marty, and Mark began to remonstrate with him. The small movements at the top of the tank of soil had become a little more telling, but still there was no sign of Arthur. It must be more than two minutes, thought Sophie. She felt strangely frozen to the spot, an observer, oddly distanced from the reality of the situation. Johnny's body language had now changed, and he pushed past Marty to the area behind the performance where the various Italian workers were collected. They quickly came up with a short ladder, brought it around to the side of the tank, where Johnny and two or three ambulance workers quickly climbed up, got into the tank and began to dig in the soil where there been some movement. Sophie had a clear view from where she was and could see that within twenty or thirty seconds they had reached Arthur, who was covered from head to toe in dirt and appeared to be immobile. One of the ambulance workers put him on his shoulder, where he hung like a sack of potatoes. Sophie could not tell whether or not he was breathing, she was too far away, but it was clear from the body language of the paramedics that the event had turned from a performance to a life-and-death situation. Arthur was now being attended to on the floor next to the tank; a stretcher suddenly appeared, and Arthur was hurriedly placed on it and rushed away by two of the paramedics holding the stretcher. It was only a short distance to the water, and Sophie could see from her vantage point that they were trotting away with Arthur on the stretcher to their water ambulance. There was obviously a great deal of urgency involved. While this was happening, Johnny and Mark were having a loud conversation with Marty, involving lots of arm waving and even a little pushing and shoving of Marty by Mark. Marty himself was then pulled by the arm by another paramedic, and they both began running in the direction of the stretcher and the ambulance. A remaining paramedic began talking to Johnny and Mark with more accompanying gesticulation. Sophie was surrounded by the horrified faces of the remaining onlookers; just below her were Henri and Caroline. The colour had drained from Henri's face as, no doubt, the full impact of what was going on started to hit him. Caroline seemed calmer. They were speaking quietly to one another in French, but Sophie could still just about make out what they were saying.

'I still think it might have been part of the show. Let's hang on to see what happens next,' Henri was saying.

'I don't want to be here when they realise that something has definitely gone very wrong,' Caroline replied. 'Look at those journalists and photographers down there. They've already got a load of photos. I don't want to be associated with this in the newspapers, particularly the British tabloids. This looks ugly, Henri. We need to make an exit.'

'Shouldn't we at least wait until there is some kind of an announcement? Look down there.' He pointed down towards

Johnny and Mark, who were deep in conversation with the remaining ambulance worker. 'They're my friends. I'd like to help them if I can.'

'You do as you wish, Henri. I'm leaving. I'll see you at the hotel.'

Sophie watched as Caroline, now armed with a fake smile, quietly filtered through the crowd and disappeared. Sophie was pretty sure that they had just witnessed a performance that had gone horribly wrong. Whether or not it was art had now become an irrelevance; Arthur's life seemed to be at stake. She walked a few steps down to join Henri, who still seemed to be computing what was happening.

'Come on, Henri, we need to go and see if we can help down there.'

Henri followed her down to where Johnny and Mark were still in a heated discussion with the paramedic. This didn't seem to be helped by the Italian's lack of English, and a corresponding dearth of Italian on the side of the Brits. Henri led Sophie through the mêlée of photographers and journalists, and they arrived next to their friends.

'What the fuck is going on, guys?' Henri said.

'He's in real trouble,' said Mark. He was on the verge of tears.

'We don't think he was breathing when they took him away,' said Johnny.

Sophie felt her chest tighten at the shock of what she was hearing.

Henri started to speak to the paramedic in Italian. While he wasn't fluent, he seemed to be able to make himself understood. They were being jostled by the group of journalists.

'What's going on, guys?'

'Is he dead?'

'Where have they taken him, Johnny?'

Johnny seemed to have been recognised. He turned to the journalists while Henri carried on in Italian. 'Can you guys shut the fuck up while we try to find out what's happening? Have some common fucking decency, will you?'

That quietened them down.

'Right,' said Henri, 'he doesn't really know exactly how Arthur is, but he does know that they've taken him to the nearest emergency hospital. It's about ten minutes by boat. Marty is with him.'

The paramedic was now on his radio. He said something to Henri in Italian.

'We need to get you a boat, Mark, then you can get to the hospital. I get the impression that this is touch and go. He seems to have been suffocating on the dirt while he was trying to burrow his way out. They're doing what they can. Let's get you on that boat.'

'I'll go with him,' said Johnny.

'Yes, of course, Johnny. We'll get back to the hotel once we've found a boat for you, so at least you know where we are.'

It sounded very serious to Sophie. She really felt for Mark. He was clearly distraught.

'I'm sure he'll be OK,' she said putting an arm around his shoulder. She had no idea whether or not she believed what she had just said.

***

The water taxi throttled down as they came up to the mooring area for the Ospedale SS. Giovanni e Paolo. Johnny spotted Marty waiting for them on one of the pontoons and asked the taxi to moor there. They hadn't said much to one another on the short journey around the north side of the lagoon; all they wanted to do was get there as soon as they could. The taxi driver had been instructed to put his foot down by Henri, and clearly he had understood the urgency of the situation. The journey had been at full pelt and had only taken a matter of minutes. They both jumped out of the boat on arrival and instinctively started to run to where Marty was waiting.

'So what's happening?' Johnny asked Marty, slowing to a jog as Marty struggled to keep up alongside.

'It's not looking good, I'm afraid.'

'What do you mean?' asked Johnny as they came off the pontoon to the entrance to the hospital.

'I think we've lost him, son,' said Marty.

'What?' Johnny couldn't believe what he was hearing.

'I think he's gone. They couldn't seem to get him breathing again. I know it's hard to take in, but I really think he's gone.'

By now they were inside the hospital and had slowed to a walk. Marty was breathing quite heavily as he directed them down a corridor to the right of the waiting area, the signs on the walls indicating that they were heading to the ambulance arrival area. Towards the end of the long corridor were two of the paramedics that Johnny recognised from the Biennale site. They were standing outside a door marked with an Italian sign that Johnny could not understand.

'He's in there.' Marty hung his head as he spoke, unable to make eye contact. 'I've done the formal identification, but you can look at him if you want to. They're waiting for the guys from the mortuary to take him away. Then apparently he'll go to a funeral director to be prepared to be flown home.'

'I don't understand, Marty. He was alive about half an hour ago. Why can't they bring him round?'

'They've tried, Mark. Believe me, they've tried. All the way here on the boat they were trying, but he didn't respond. He was under that soil for too long.'

'Well, they should have fucking tried harder.'

'Do you want to go and see him?' asked Johnny.

'No, I can't bear it. You go if you want to.'

Something in Johnny wanted to make sure that Arthur really was dead and that this was not some kind of elaborate hoax; he knew he was in a state of shock but was trying to behave as rationally as he could for Mark's sake.

'I'll go and see him,' he said to Marty. This wish was conveyed to the paramedics by Marty in broken Italian. One of them went into the room then called Johnny in a few seconds later. He walked in. The room was empty other than for a couple of chairs and a metal trolley, which clearly had a body on it covered by a sheet. There was a pile of muddied black clothes lying against the wall and a pair of black steel toe cap boots next to them also plastered with the soil from the tank. Without saying anything the paramedic pulled the sheet away to reveal a dead, naked Arthur. There was no doubt in Johnny's mind that he was dead; his head lolled to one side and was covered in the mud that had suffocated him. The dirt stopped at the neckline where his black T-shirt would have been; below his collar bone his hairy body was revealed in an unnaturally stark way. It was shocking to see such a young man's corpse like this, inert on a slab. The image of *Dead Dad* at *Sensation* flashed into his mind; the inert nakedness of the artwork had somehow prepared him for this moment. In any case, he had seen enough.

He walked back into the corridor where Mark was remonstrating with Marty. 'What the fuck were you doing letting him try this ridiculous stunt?'

'I'm sorry, Mark. I did warn him about the risks, but you know what he was like. He wouldn't listen. His mind was made up.'

'And now he's fucking dead. Because of you, Marty.'

'I'm very sorry, Mark, but I can confirm that he is dead. It's definitely him, and he's definitely gone,' Johnny interrupted Mark.

Johnny heard his phone ringing. He looked, and it was Sophie. He moved away a few paces.

'What's happening, Johnny? Are you there yet?'

'We're at the hospital. He's gone, babe. He died on the way. I've just seen his body.'

'Oh my God. I can't believe it, Johnny. How's Mark?'

'Not good. He's having a proper go at Marty.'

'I don't blame him.'

'I think I need to get Mark out of here. I'll tell Marty to deal with all the paperwork. It's the least he can do after what has happened. I'll get Mark back to the hotel. We'll see you there.'

THE AFTERMATH

1999

Henri lay in Caroline's bed in the Old Town in Geneva. She had gone to the bathroom after they had made love. Their lovemaking now followed a familiar pattern. She would be on top, then, as she became more and more aroused, she would smack him hard on the cheek a couple of times. To his later embarrassment, this would arouse him until they both climaxed, normally, she first and he shortly afterwards. There was then very little, if any, post-coital intimacy before Caroline either turned over and went to sleep or went to the bathroom for an extended period before coming back and going straight to sleep. Either way, Henri was left alone in contemplation, as the moment of sexual pleasure passed, and his stinging cheek reminded him of the guilt and awkwardness he felt about letting himself be abused in this way. He had intended to come to Geneva to finish things with her. Her behaviour after Arthur's tragic death in Venice had really made him think about her decency; while he himself prided himself on his pragmatic and unsentimental attitude to life, he liked to believe that left room for doing the right thing at the right time. He had been unable to come to terms with how Caroline had slipped away as she saw Arthur dying in front of her own eyes, her only thoughts being about self-preservation. She had also avoided his friends as they had regrouped back at the Ca'Sagredo immediately following the tragedy. Mark had been in pieces as the reality of what had just happened began to sink in. He had pinned a lot of the blame on Marty, who had also been notable by his absence, but Henri knew that Caroline had encouraged Arthur in his desire to perform live, as she had thought that the publicity was a wonderful thing. She now knew at first hand how unpleasant life could be in the face of the British tabloid press; the extreme personal intrusion of their reporting had largely missed Caroline directly, as most of their vitriol had fallen on the 'faceless' bureaucrats at the British Council, who had been the tabloids' scapegoats for allowing Arthur's fatal performance to take place. They were camped outside Galerie Schmidt in Hoxton, however – although Caroline had largely chosen to ignore this. A few of them had also found their way to Galerie Schmidt in Geneva, and their proximity had unsettled her enough to temporarily hire some security at the door to the gallery. Two large, uniformed security guards standing outside the gallery door in the ultra-conservative Old Town were not a great look. Being based in Paris and Geneva, they were both somewhat cushioned from the furore in the UK media in the wake of Arthur's death, but the funeral was in a few days' time, and they knew that there would be another round of blame calling and condemnation when that took place. He hadn't asked Caroline if she was going to attend; if they were going to split up it didn't really matter to him one way or the other. Anyway, he would leave that conversation to the morning. He felt uncomfortable that he hadn't been able to talk to her immediately after making love one last time, but he would definitely do so when they woke up.

The next morning Henri sat nursing his coffee in Caroline's small but perfectly formed kitchen. He would have liked to have lit his first Disque Bleu of the day, it might have settled his nerves, but he was banned from smoking in her apartment. He was starting to rehearse his lines in his head as he sipped on the coffee.

'So, have you made your travel arrangements for the funeral

next week?' Henri was a little surprised that she was asking him. He had assumed that she would try to avoid it.

'I was going to go by train from Paris, but I haven't booked anything yet.'

'Can you book me a ticket, too? I feel like I should go.'

'Really? I didn't think you would.'

'I've thought about it since Venice, and I think I made a mistake there, leaving the event early and avoiding the aftermath. I think I need to face up to what happened, and going to the funeral will help me to do that. I'd like to be with you and your friends, too. I know how hard it's been on them, particularly Mark.'

'I'm surprised. I'm pleased, but I'm surprised.'

'We all have to face the world, *mon amour.* There is no point hiding. I realise that now.'

'It's good to hear you say that,' said Henri, mentally cancelling the conversation he had been about to have. 'I'll make the bookings for us. The service is at a church in Shoreditch. I'll book a hotel nearby.'

'Do you think they might like to use the gallery for the drinks afterwards?'

'I can ask Mark. I think he's booked somewhere else. I'm not sure how he'll feel about having the drinks at your gallery. I'm not sure what he thinks about our role in what happened. I'll call him today. I feel pretty bad myself that we didn't try to do more to find out exactly what Arthur was going to try to attempt.'

She was full of surprises, Caroline. Her change in attitude was not enough to change his mind about their relationship, however, but now he would wait until after the funeral before he brought it to a close.

***

Johnny had thought that a beer in the Compton Arms might help Mark get through another difficult day. He hadn't seen him since they had left Venice, and he was now sitting in their regular haunt nursing a pint of London Pride waiting for his oldest friend. He knew today was the day that Arthur's body was arriving back in the UK from Italy because Marty had already told him about all the things he had had to do to arrange it: obtain an Italian death certificate and have that translated to English; take the translation to a register office and get a UK death certificate; organise a funeral director in the UK to receive the body; then organise for the body to be flown from Italy to London. Arthur was arriving home today and would be picked up from the airport by Hampton & Everly Funeral Directors in Hoxton. They would hold the body until the funeral service next week.

Johnny himself had managed to rearrange the remainder of his tour, with gigs not restarting until after the funeral. It had become common knowledge through the newspapers that Johnny had been friends with Arthur and that he had halted the tour for a while as a mark of respect, having been a witness to his awful death. Somehow the papers had also managed to work out that Johnny's estranged father had also been involved, and while Marty had been lying low, thereby avoiding a lot of the flack, some of the bad publicity was starting to rub off on Johnny. The tabloids, in particular, seemed to be looking for a scapegoat for Arthur's demise, and Marty now seemed to be one of the candidates; by association, this also seemed to mean that Johnny had been involved somehow. Even though Johnny was, in his own eyes, a pretty minor celebrity, he was famous enough for the tabloids to take a lot of interest, and, while they weren't doorstepping him in East Sussex, he had stopped bothering to answer his phone, which had been plagued by calls and voicemails. Fuck the papers, he thought, they've always been arseholes. He would do his best to ignore them. Marty had gone to ground. He had told Johnny he would be back in touch for the funeral, but in the meantime he would be out of circulation and uncontactable.

Mark walked into the pub wearing his work suit. He'd told Johnny on the phone that he had gone back to work in an attempt to keep busy.

'Mate, how are you doing?' He gave Mark a big hug.

'I'm OK, Johnny, but I really need to get this funeral out of the way. I'm dreading it.'

Johnny went to the bar and came back with a pint of bitter for Mark.

'Would you believe, Henri called me today, making an offer on Caroline's behalf to use Galerie Schmidt in Hoxton for the wake. I'm not sure how to take it, to be honest. We were going to do something at Arthur's studio. They're both right near Shoreditch Church, so they're both easy to get to afterwards. What do you think?'

'I'm not sure, mate.' It seemed to have been a rhetorical question from Mark anyway, as he carried on speaking.

'I suppose she feels guilty by association about what happened and is trying to be nice, but I'm not sure it's an appropriate venue. Part of me thinks that it should be a pretty sombre affair, but I don't think of the gallery as a sombre place, then another part of me thinks it should be a wild, joyous affair to reflect Arthur's nature. He could be grumpy and difficult at times, but he loved life. I'm not sure he would have wanted sombre. On the plus side, using the gallery would mean that I have less to do, as Henri told me that they would take care of everything, including all the catering. That does appeal to me, I must admit. I've tried to discuss it with Arthur's parents, but they're in a bit of state. Not only have they lost their only child but they're going to have to come down to London for the funeral. They've both lived in Scunthorpe all their lives, and they don't travel much. His mum's a primary school teacher, and his dad's a civil servant. It's a big deal for them to go to Leeds, so this is all a bit much.'

It was a bit of a stream of consciousness, which was unusual for Mark. He was normally more considered.

'You know, I think you should have it at the gallery. It's kind of in keeping with Arthur's world, and it takes a load of hassle off your plate.'

'Well, that's what I was coming around to thinking.'

They sat for a while drinking and talking about the arrangements.

'Are you going back to Brede tonight?' Mark asked. 'You're welcome to stay at my place if you want to. I could do with the company, to be honest.'

'Sure. I don't have to be home tonight. I'll call Sophie to let her know.'

An hour or so later they were sipping Lagavulin on Mark's sofa back at the flat overlooking Highbury Fields. Johnny felt deeply sorry for his friend and ex-lover. It was clear that, although his relationship with Arthur had only been relatively short, Mark was deeply upset by his passing.

'If only he had told me what he was going to do, I could have stopped him. I've been over it so many times. I just needed to warn him of the risks. He should never have been thinking of gambling his life for the sake of his art, but that was him all over. The art meant more than anything to him, and authenticity was one of his big things. He would have wanted the stunt to have been real with no fakery.'

Mark began to cry quietly. In all the time they had been friends, since the first year at the grammar school together, he had never seen Mark cry. Instinctively he put his arm around Mark's shoulders.

'I'm sorry, mate,' Mark began to apologise.

'Don't worry, man,' Johnny replied, 'just let it out.'

And Mark did let it out. He cried in Johnny's arms for a long time. When he had finally stopped crying, Mark started to kiss Johnny on the mouth, hard, almost like a plea for intimacy. Johnny felt himself responding. He had thought they had moved past this kind of physicality, but he still felt that urge. For Mark's sake he would not try to fight it.

***

Sophie answered her phone and was surprised to hear Henri at the other end. Earlier that day she had again wondered if she had been a little too tough on him when he had tried to confide in her in Venice. That conversation had been rather overtaken by events, so she had put it to the back of her mind, but it was a coincidence that it had resurfaced just before he called.

'Hi, Sophie. Can you talk?'

'Yes. Amy's in bed, and Johnny just called to say he's staying at Mark's tonight. Mark's still pretty upset by the sound of it.'

'I'm not surprised.' There was a short silence.

'I'm still pretty knocked sideways by the whole thing, *bouleversé*, as you guys would say.'

'Are you going to the funeral next week?'

'Yes, of course.'

'I've just got back from Geneva.'

'To see her royal highness, no doubt. Is she still slapping you? She was notable by her absence when it all kicked off in Venice, by the way. It was almost as if she was avoiding us.' Sophie cringed a little listening to herself. She was maybe weighing in a little too much.

'I know her behaviour in Venice was inexplicable. But yes, I was seeing Caroline in Geneva. Between the two of us, I went to see her to finish it, but it didn't happen. I couldn't bring myself to do it.'

'She really has emasculated you, hasn't she, Henri? I wish you had shown that kind of consideration when we were seeing each other.'

'I'm sorry, Sophie. I let you down.'

'Well, thank you. I really appreciate you saying that.'

'I know. I've been doing a lot of thinking since Arthur died. I know I can be insensitive and selfish, but I think Caroline is even more so than I am. The way she behaved opened my eyes to it. If you can't rely on the people who are supposed to be close to you in a situation like that, when can you? It left me feeling rather hollow.'

'It's good to hear you say that, Henri. Don't worry, I thought you behaved admirably, despite Caroline's disappearance. You were a real help to Mark.'

'Thanks. Caroline has decided to come to the funeral with me. That's why I have put off finishing with her. We'll go to that, and then I'll call it a day.'

'Really? I would have thought that would be the last place she would want to be. Does she know the British tabloids will be there? Maybe even the French ones, too. The story hasn't quite gone cold over here.'

'Yes, she knows. She feels bad, and she wants to make amends. She has offered the gallery in Hoxton to Mark for the wake as a goodwill gesture.'

'Has she? Well, that is actually good of her. Has Mark taken her up on the offer?'

'Not yet, but I think he will.' There was a silence, then Henri continued, 'It's good to talk to you, Sophie, even if you are still giving me a hard time. I am going to break things off with Caroline, not just because she slaps me but because I realise now that she's not that nice a person. I thought I was the only shark in the water. I now realise there are plenty of others, and I'm spending too much time with one of them.'

Sophie smiled to herself. 'Well, that might be hard to admit to yourself, Henri. I'm glad you are starting to find the real you.'

'Is that what's happening?' Henri began to laugh. 'I'm not sure I've got quite that far yet, but thanks for the encouragement. I'll see you next week. I'll be with Caroline, but at least you now know it will not be for much longer.'

'I'll see you then. Take care.'

As she put the phone down Sophie felt herself welling up a little. She had put on a tough act, but it had been quite difficult. She had never known Henri be quite as vulnerable as he had been in their last two conversations. Before he started seeing Caroline he had been so confident, arrogant even, and that had been part of his appeal. She had never been in love with him, she realised now, but definitely in lust for a little while. She was glad that his unequal relationship with Caroline had taught him some lessons; maybe he had flown too close to the sun and was now paying the price. Interesting that he had used the shark metaphor; she remembered him telling her how much he had admired Damien Hirst's work at the *Sensation* exhibition. She had thought of this at the time as a window into his mind, an indication of how he thought of himself, alone, speeding through the water in search of his prey, a man in constant motion at the top of the food chain. He now knew that this could be a lonely place. She found it hard to decipher the emotion that she felt. Was it driven by empathy, or even sympathy, for Henri, or was it more to do with her own gratitude that he had finally realised that he had not behaved well towards her? Whatever the explanation, she felt better about what had happened between them.

***

Mark had woken early at his flat after a fitful night's sleep. The day he was dreading had arrived all too quickly, and he felt sick to the bottom of his stomach. Thankfully, the funeral service was going to be relatively early, at 10 a.m., so the most difficult part of the day would be out of the way by around lunchtime. The wake would follow at the gallery in Hoxton Square. Mark was hoping that this might be a little easier. Arthur's parents had wanted a church ceremony, so he and Marty had simply asked the church nearest to Arthur's studio if they would do it. This was St Leonards on Shoreditch High Street, where, Mark felt, at least Arthur would have appreciated the history of the site. While he hadn't been religious, he had an understanding of history and had respected the way that all religions marked important moments with ritual. He had also had a great deal of respect for his parents, despite the lack of commonality in the way they all led their lives, and Mark felt strongly that Arthur would have wanted his parents' views respected for a funeral service. He had helped them find a hotel near the church, and while he had only met them a couple of times, and then never officially as Arthur's partner, he, too, found them to be decent, modest people who had been rather shocked by Arthur's newfound fame.

He had hoped that Johnny might stay with him last night, it being the night before the funeral, but Johnny had retreated a little since their night together the previous week. Mark himself was a little confused by what had happened; he felt responsible somehow for drawing Johnny back into a physical relationship, but he had needed the intimacy to assuage his grief. He hadn't felt guilty or felt that he should have had more respect for Arthur's passing. Arthur had not been one for jealousy or guilt; life was for living, and if you felt an instinctive response to something, you should follow your instincts. It was less the fact that he and Johnny had had sex and more the emotional element that he found confusing; he understood how grief might make you seek out physical closeness, but why Johnny? Familiarity perhaps? Maybe there was something latent there, something he thought had passed. Typically for them, once it was over and the night had passed they had not discussed what had happened, even when they had woken that morning in the same bed. Nor had they discussed it when they chatted on the phone about the funeral. This could have been because Johnny was at home with his family and had not been able to talk, but Mark knew better than that. It had left him feeling very alone, with the weight of his grief for Arthur heavy on his shoulders. Work helped, keeping busy helped, but he needed to mark Arthur's passing today so he could take the first day of the rest of his life without him.

***

'So why can't they come again?'

'I just don't think they wanted to in the end. They didn't really know Arthur. It's quite a lot of effort and expense to come over, and I told Juste that I'd be OK with you. We'd look after one another.'

'How convinced was she by that? She's not my greatest fan after all, is she?'

There was a sudden jolt as their cab driver braked too abruptly in the Strand. It was a relatively short cab ride up to Shoreditch from Charing Cross where they had got off the train.

'I think the more she's got to know you the more she likes you. Anyway, I thought you might have stayed with Mark last night. Was he on his own?'

'As far as I know. I thought about offering, but he seems to be doing pretty well.' Johnny shifted in his seat as he told the white lie. Fortunately, they were sitting side by side on the back seat, so his unease was not so obvious. He could tell when chatting to Mark by phone that he was not doing well.

'Really? I'm surprised. I think he genuinely loved Arthur, you know. I'm sure he's not going to get over what happened in just a few days.'

'Yes, I know, you're right. What I meant was, he's doing pretty well, all things considered.'

'To be honest, you sound like you're trying to convince yourself that he's OK. Let's look out for him today, in any case. It was bad enough watching what happened as a friend, never mind if it was happening to your partner.'

'You're right. We should look out for him.'

'I told you I spoke to Henri, didn't I?'

'Yes, you did. You thought he sounded a bit weird.'

'Definitely. Like he'd had the stuffing knocked out of him. Let's look out for him today, too. And how about Marty? Any word?'

'Incognito. He's not answering his phone. I'm sure he'll be there.'

'I'm not going to suggest we look out for *him*. I think he's done well enough on his own all these years. What about the press? What are you expecting?'

'I'm expecting there to be a full turn out. I know it's disappeared from the front pages, but a funeral always stirs them up. I think Mark has hired security to keep them out of the church.'

***

As soon as they pulled up to the entrance to the church the press were on them. Sophie braced herself. As Johnny had predicted there were security guards on hand forming a protective wall between them and the vultures of Fleet Street. They shouted questions:

'How are you feeling, Johnny? Couldn't you have stopped him doing it?'

'Your dad must be feeling bad. Why didn't you stop them, Johnny?'

The press had been looking for a scapegoat since the performance in Venice. The official verdict was that it had been a terrible accident and that Arthur had performed the stunt at his own risk. The Italian authorities were apparently not interested in taking matters any further, as it was clearly death by misadventure. There had been rumblings in the press about the responsibility of the British Council to their chosen artist, but these seemed to have petered out. Most people now accepted that Arthur had wanted to perform the stunt; he had set it up, and it had simply gone wrong. Johnny hadn't been able to quiz Marty about how much safety planning they had done, but the fact that there were paramedics on the site showed Arthur knew the risks he was taking. Sophie still had flashbacks to the moment when they knew that something bad had happened, the stirring on the surface of the soil in that fateful glass tank, the appearance of Arthur's limp body, his face covered in dirt, and the panic in the eyes of Marty and the paramedics.

Johnny took her hand as they were ushered into the church. Columns running down the nave supported a gallery. The wooden pews at ground level were already nearly full. Marty stood at the far end in front of the altar, and he motioned to them to come to the front. As they walked down the aisle Sophie felt a little self-conscious, gripping Johnny's hand tightly. Her outfit now felt somewhat ostentatiously funereal; she had chosen a black, veiled pillbox hat to go with her vintage black skirt-suit and black stilettos. She realised now, belatedly, that it probably looked a little too *Godfather.* As they moved down the church she could see that Shoreditch's contemporary artists had come out in force. She found it comforting seeing Tracey and gave her a discreet wave; Tracey smiled back. The artist crowd were all dressed in bright primary colours, perhaps deliberately, with splashes of white, almost like a Mondrian. As they arrived at the front of the church Marty pointed to the second row from the front on the right, where Sophie could already see Henri and Caroline installed. They greeted one another with silent hugs. They were both wearing black, too: Caroline, a black sleeveless dress with a high neck reminiscent of the late Princess Diana; Henri, an immaculate charcoal suit, white shirt and black silk tie. She sat down next to Caroline not knowing if they should speak or if that would be inappropriate. She had little experience of funerals and felt a little awkward; she had liked Arthur and was still in a state of shock over his death, but she did not feel upset to the point of tears. She glanced to her right, where Caroline wore her usual unemotional mask across her handsome but inexpressive face; next to her, Henri sat looking ahead, his jaw a little clenched, lost in his own thoughts. She took Johnny's hand, and he turned and smiled an encouraging smile. Just as she did so Mark appeared in the central aisle accompanied by an elderly couple, whom she assumed were Arthur's parents. As they went to sit down in the pew in front, Johnny got up to greet them. He gave Mark a big hug and shook Arthur's parents' hands, expressing his condolences. Sophie looked on and gave Mark what she hoped was a warm and sympathetic smile. She watched as Johnny tried to help put his bereaved friend at ease. Johnny was a good man; he had his faults, but he was a good man. Just ahead of Johnny and in front of the altar was a metal bier, presumably waiting to support the coffin when it arrived.

'You'll get one number and one number only, because I'm a lazy bastard.' Without warning, the church PA had come to life. Sophie recognised the voice. Then immediately the Sex Pistols' cover of the Stooges' 'No Fun' began blasting out. It was a pretty ramshackle version and an odd way to start a funeral but, somehow, very Arthur. Mark must have chosen it. As the distorted guitar reverberated around the old building and they listened to Johnny Rotten telling whoever would listen that it was '*no fun*', Sophie saw people beginning to look over their shoulders as the pall-bearers began their slow progress down the aisle with the coffin on their shoulders. The music should have been incongruous, but Sophie felt it was a perfect fit; being at a funeral was not any fun, and it was even less fun for the sadly departed Arthur. The vicar had now appeared and stood in front of the altar, waiting for the coffin. The Sex Pistols continued to ring out as the pall-bearers placed the coffin on the bier; as they finished, the music shambled to a close with Rotten's repeated cries of '*no fun*' rebounding off the church walls. The pall-bearers moved away from the coffin as the music finally stopped and all that could be heard in the silence around the church was Rotten's parting shot: 'Ever get the feeling you've been cheated?'

Very Arthur, thought Sophie. She turned and smiled at Johnny, who smiled back, enjoying the irony.

With that famous quote ringing in their ears, the Sex Pistols gave way to a hubbub among the congregation as an unexpected banging sound started up. It took Sophie a moment to work out where it was coming from. It was a muffled, thudding sound. The vicar had moved towards his microphone to make his opening address but stepped back looking extremely perturbed by the noise. Sophie rapidly realised that the banging sound was coming from the coffin.

'What the fuck is that?' said Johnny, definitely loudly enough for the vicar to hear. There were shouts and screams now as the hubbub turned into a racket. Sophie watched horrified as the vicar walked down from the altar to inspect the coffin, and the pall-bearers marched back down the aisle. Right on cue, the 'foot' end of the coffin burst open, and a familiar pair of steel toe cap boots appeared, swiftly followed by the unmistakeable, black clad form of Arthur Swale. Marty had simultaneously taken over the vicar's microphone. As Arthur bowed to his assembled friends and family, Marty made an announcement: 'And that, my friends, brings an end to the performance of *The Histrionic* personality type, which began in Venice at the opening of Arthur's exhibition. We hope you are more amused than alarmed by this performance. Arthur welcomes you all to his own wake, which will now follow at Galerie Schmidt in Hoxton Square.'

Arthur continued to bow with a large grin on his face, and some people had begun to clap, but all in all it was a mixed response to what had been an enormous shock.

How could he have put his parents through this, thought Sophie?

'You fucking idiots,' she heard Johnny say. She couldn't have put it better herself.

***

As Arthur bowed to what he obviously considered an audience, Henri noticed that Caroline had a wide smile on her face as she looked on. The penny dropped immediately. He knew that smile; it was one of self-satisfaction. She had known all along what Arthur was up to. She may have even been involved in cooking up the stunt in the first place.

'*Putain*,' he said to her in French. 'You knew. You knew he wasn't dead. In Venice, in Geneva, right up until now, you knew it was all a stunt, and you kept it to yourself. That's why you offered the gallery for the wake, because you knew it was going to be a party not a wake.'

'There may be some truth in that suggestion.' Caroline was clearly proud of herself.

'Have you thought about Arthur's parents? They thought they were coming to their son's funeral. Mark thought he had lost his partner.' Henri was trying to stay calm, but he knew he had begun to raise his voice. Fortunately, there was quite a furore going on around him to cover it up.

'I imagine Arthur would say that without suffering there is no art. Sometimes it is not only the artist who has to suffer.'

'Well, I'll let you explain that to the people who loved Arthur.'

'We all love Arthur, Henri. I'm surprised you are being such a killjoy.'

'I'm not sure that I see much joy in a man faking his own death.'

'It was a performance. Think of the publicity. There are a whole crowd of journalists waiting right outside. This should become an international story. Arthur's name will reach heights that we never dreamed of.'

By now there was a crowd of people around Arthur. Henri noticed that Arthur's parents, together with Mark, had remained seated in the pew in front. He slipped out of his seat to see how they were. The conversation with Caroline could wait. His morality had been severely tested recently, and he was beginning to realise that he was not quite as hardnosed and ambitious as he had previously thought; it had taken exposure to Caroline's ambition at all costs to appreciate that there were limits to his own. He sat down next to Mark, who was looking down at his feet as if he had had the stuffing knocked out of him.

'How are you doing, Mark?' he asked.

'I'm not sure I'll ever be able to forgive him for this,' he replied.

'It's only just happened. You might want to let it sink in before you draw any permanent conclusions.'

'I know, I realise that, but look next to us.' Mark lowered his voice. 'Never mind me, I'll get over it, and it is wonderful that Arthur is alive, when I thought he was dead, but look at those two.'

Henri looked at Arthur's parents sitting the other side of Mark. They were probably in their sixties, with an out-of-town look that stood out in London. Arthur's mother was crying silently into a handkerchief, while his father had a protective arm around her and a stern look on his face. They were hardly celebrating their son's Lazarus act.

'Are you going to the gallery?' he asked Mark.

'I'm not sure. I'm emotionally exhausted, to be honest. I'm not sure I'm up to it.'

'Well, you can come with us. I'll find out if Johnny and Sophie are going.'

'OK, then maybe I will, if you're all going. I need to speak to Arthur first, but I'm going to have to wait for his cheerleaders to disappear.'

They looked over where Arthur was still surrounded by friends, largely the artist community of Shoreditch that Henri recognised, patting him on the back, laughing and whooping. They were clearly buzzed by what had happened. He turned behind to see Caroline watching on, still standing in the pew, perhaps as happy as he had ever seen her.

***

'So how the fuck did you manage to pull that off?'

Johnny had finally managed to take Marty to one side. He had left Sophie with Henri and Mark, both of whom seemed to have taken a dim view of what Arthur had put them through. He had a welcome beer in one hand and a Marlboro Light in the other, which were helping him recover from the shock of Arthur kicking his way out of his own coffin.

'Believe it or not, son, it was pretty straightforward.' Johnny raised his eyebrows. 'The most difficult part was sorting out the ambulance guys in Venice. In the end we just went for an uncomplicated bribe. The guys you saw were real paramedics, being paid by us to follow our instructions. I had an old artist contact in Venice who helped put us in touch with them. They quite liked the irreverence of what we were doing. Still wanted their palms greased, though. Anyway, we knew Arthur could get out of the coffin with the right kind of soil in the tank. It's a trick Houdini tried and only just managed to pull off, but he had been six feet down. Arthur wasn't as far down. The coffin he was in had a false end, a bit like the one at the funeral. Once he'd kicked it out, he just had to push his way up through the soil.'

'Just…'

'Well, in actual fact, it was quite easy to do that because of the type of soil we'd chosen; it was very light and sandy. In the end he stayed under a bit longer than he needed to just to make it look more realistic.'

'How did you get him into the mortuary at the hospital.?'

'It wasn't a mortuary, it was just a room in the hospital, conveniently close to the entrance. When you came in to identify him, he just held his breath and tried to play dead. We were relying on the fact that you wouldn't be in there for long because you were so shocked. Did you realise you were only in there for about thirty seconds? Playing dead for that long was a piece of cake.' Johnny shook his head in disbelief. 'I had to hang around a bit to make sure I got the Italian death certificate, but Arthur just got on a train. Milan, Paris, London. He just wore a hat and kept his head down.'

'How did you get the death certificate if he wasn't dead and there was no body?'

'Well, the paramedics helped us with that. Again, money talks. All I needed was a piece of paper that looked right to show the Brits. We just bought a forged Italian death certificate. Once I had that I registered the death in the UK so I could then show the vicar and the funeral people the right bit of paper.'

'So where was Arthur?' The story seemed so ludicrously simple.

'He was holed up at my place in Hackney. He went a bit stir crazy, but it was worth it.'

'So how did he get into the coffin for the funeral.'

'Again, we had someone on the inside. Arthur knew a guy who worked there, just from drinking in the local pubs around here. The guy wants to be an artist and works at the funeral directors to pay the rent. We had a fake coffin with a lump of plaster of Paris in it delivered to the funeral people, which was enough to fool them into thinking it was the body flown back from Italy. I told them not to open the coffin because the body had already been prepared. As you now know, there was a false end in this one, too. With the help of our accomplice, we sneaked Arthur in first thing this morning and took the lump of plaster out. He was only in there a couple of hours. Uncomfortable but not life threatening.'

Marty was so matter of fact about it all.

'So whose idea was it?'

'It was Arthur's. He's the ideas man.'

'And what about all the people who thought he was dead? His parents, Mark, his close friends?'

'He didn't give much of a toss about that, to be honest. It's art, son. Arthur lives it. Nothing else matters. He sees it as the ultimate piece of performance art. Successfully faking your own death. Who else has ever pulled that off? No other artist in history.'

'I sat with Mark last week crying his eyes out.'

'He should be happy now then, because Arthur's not dead.'

'Did anyone else know?'

'Caroline Schmidt knew. Arthur discussed it with her. She thought it was a great idea apparently.'

'Why am I not surprised?'

'I think it's a triumph, son. He'll be remembered for ever more. This takes him to the next level.'

'And that's what's important?'

'If you're an artist, yes. You want people to appreciate your work. You want to be recognised. You want to move people, to affect them in a way that they remember.'

Johnny was confused. He understood the need to be recognised and loved, but surely this had taken things too far. He could tell Marty was never going to agree with him. He lit another cigarette. His father was a conundrum; plenty of strident opinions but a lack of empathy and compassion. The man who had been dead to him all those years was now alive to him, and he was not sure that he liked what he had found.

***

Mark and Sophie sat next to one another on one of the chic white leather-and-steel sofas at the gallery. They were both sipping on glasses of champagne, but somehow Mark found the celebratory nature of the drink inappropriate. They had been sitting for a while in a shocked silence that Mark at least found somehow comforting. Arthur's parents had left straight after the funeral – or the performance, as it now seemed to be termed – taking the train straight back to Scunthorpe. His father had explained that it was not their crowd. Mark realised that they were probably used to Arthur's wild ideas; even so he could tell that they were doing their best to conceal the emotional rollercoaster they had been on.

He and Sophie looked on as Arthur continued to hold court at the centre of an admiring group of artist friends. It looked as if a handful of journalists and photographers had infiltrated the wake. Nobody cared now that all had been revealed. There was no longer any need for the papers to blame anyone for Arthur's death because he was not dead. He supposed that Arthur's assumption now would be that he would be praised for pulling off such a stunt. However, Mark knew the tabloids were never on anyone's side for very long; the more Arthur used them to increase his profile, the further he would fall when they chose to dethrone him. He was playing with fire. They had hugged briefly in the church, but he had felt limp and unimportant in Arthur's arms.

'I'm not sure that I can go back to him, Sophie. He's shown me such a lack of respect. I'm not even sure that I'm pleased that he's still alive.'

'Love does funny things to us, Mark. Look at Johnny and me. We've overcome a few difficulties.'

Mark realised immediately that she was referring to him and Johnny and how humiliated Sophie herself had felt seeing them together in Brede. It had not quite been a life-and-death situation, but he now had a better understanding of how she had felt.

'Yes, I know, and I'm sorry.' And he *was* sorry. Despite the recent rekindling of his on–off affair with Johnny, he was still sorry about how this made Sophie feel. She was right. Love did strange things to you.

'You think we might be able to get through this then?'

'Only if you really want to, and only if you are prepared to accept Arthur for what he is. It's not a coincidence that his first important work was called *The Narcissist* or that he will become notorious for a work called *The Histrionic*.'

Mark managed a smile, and Sophie began to laugh. They looked again at the crowd around Arthur. He was entertaining them, gesticulating and laughing, histrionic to the last. Mark noticed Henri and Caroline on the fringes; Caroline was smiling her slightly forced smile, while Henri looked on, somehow on the periphery, lacking his normal confident demeanour.

'I can't really face him yet. I'm going to hang around until it thins out, then I'll try to talk to him without the crowds. I'll see where that takes us. What are you and Johnny going to do?'

'We have to get back this afternoon for Amy, then Johnny goes back on tour tomorrow, and I'm back to the shop. Back to normal, although, after this it'll take a while for things to seem normal again.'

Normal for Mark had stopped at the *Sensation* exhibition two years previously, when Arthur had opened his eyes to that extraordinary Chapman Brothers sculpture. It had taught him to think more laterally, not to assume the obvious, not to accept things for what they might seem. The last few weeks had been an exercise in that, but what did he want for the future? Back to his own rather boring normality or the extreme highs and lows of life with Arthur Swale? Right now, boring normality seemed an attractive proposition.

***

'Can I talk to you somewhere privately?' Henri said quietly into Caroline's ear.

'Of course, *mon amour*.'

They moved away from the crowd around Arthur to a corner of the gallery, where some of Damien Hirst's spot paintings were hanging. The brighter-coloured spots leaped from the canvases, almost knowingly winking at him.

'You see, Arthur is the hero of the hour. The publicity from this will be incredible!'

'I'm pleased for you.'

'It's not just for me, *mon amour*, it's for you, too. We're all going to make money out of this. And it's not just the money, the publicity for the new gallery will be amazing. This will make Papa eat his words.'

'I don't think your papa is ever going to understand contemporary art. Even if he does, he'll be too stubborn to admit that you backed the right thing.'

'Sadly, you are probably right. Enough of Papa, he'll never be satisfied. What was it you wanted to discuss?'

Henri had not been looking forward to this moment. 'It's quite difficult, but this whole faked-death thing has given clarity to something I've been thinking about for a while now.'

'*Oui*. OK.'

'It's about us Caroline. I don't think I'm the right guy for you.'

'Of course you are. Don't be ridiculous. I know you're the right guy for me. We think the same, we want the same things, we even like the same things in the bedroom.'

'We're not the same, Caroline. I could never have let this faked death go ahead if I had known. The people around Arthur are devastated, happy that he's still alive maybe, but emotionally wrung out. Think of his elderly parents.'

'They still have their son.'

'This is a step too far for me, and it has made me realise that we are morally unsuited.'

'Listen to yourself. Morally unsuited! Henri le Cerf, the tough-talking banker, the ambitious businessman who can't take an artist's joke. You're being ridiculous, Henri. It's not like you to be so emotional.'

'I know that. I'm surprised, too, but it's over Caroline. I can't be around you any more. I'm sorry to be so direct, but it seems to be the only way to make you listen.'

'You're going to regret this, Henri.'

'That may be so, but it's a risk I'm prepared to take.'

'Well, fuck you then. And don't come crying back.'

With that Caroline turned her well-dressed back on him; he

watched as she walked away, her elegant figure, her high heels, her connections, her breeding, all disappearing from his life. She strode purposefully over to Arthur, interrupting him in full flow, to kiss him on both cheeks and tell him she was leaving. She then headed straight for the exit. She looked as if she was simply saying her goodbyes before moving on to the next meeting. Henri knew that Caroline was the master of burying her emotions and moving forward. While she might shed a tear on the way home, he was not expecting to hear any more from her; she had given him the chance in their short conversation to retract what he had said. It would surprise him if she gave him another chance. He would not see her on the train to Paris, as he knew she had to go straight back to Geneva. At least he had avoided a last, public slap around the face. The deed was done. He, too, would have to move on.

The crowd around Arthur had thinned out a little, so Johnny took the chance to approach.

'You northern twat,' he said loudly to Arthur.

'You southern prick,' Arthur rejoined.

They then hugged heartily.

'So did you know it was me when I came in to identify the body in Venice?' Johnny asked.

'Of course I fuckin' did. I hadn't gone deaf, although there was quite a lot of soil in my ears. I could hear you talking to Marty.'

'How the fuck did you pull it off?'

'Meticulous planning and attention to detail.'

'I still can't quite believe it.'

'That's what everyone's saying. I thought it might all create a bit of a stir, but even I'm a bit surprised at the interest in what happened. The journos are telling me that it's an international story.'

'What kind of a tone are they taking?'

'I've no clue. At least they'll have to stop trying to blame people for me dying. I didn't like that part of the reporting. If I want to pull a stunt like this it's my choice. No one else should be blamed if it goes wrong. Anyway, I don't really give a fuck about the press, Johnny.' He said this a little more quietly, out of earshot of any remaining reporters, so he obviously did give a fuck about them, thought Johnny. They moved away a little from the remaining gaggle of people.

'Marty's told me about all the logistics. Like I said, I still can't really believe it. I genuinely thought you were dead. There was no doubt in my mind.'

Arthur grinned at him. 'I've told the press. The British Council will have to reopen the British Pavilion at the Biennale. You know it's been closed because of all this. Nobody's seen the other nine sculptures yet, but, as we keep saying, the last few weeks have just been an extended opening ceremony.'

'I suppose that's what you intended?'

'Yeah. I always saw the whole thing as a performance. The longest performance I've ever done.' Arthur chuckled to himself.

'You know that this is what you'll always be known for.'

'If it is, that's fine. I don't give much of a fuck about what other people think.'

'Have you had time to talk to Mark yet?' Johnny asked. 'He was in bits, you know, when he thought you were dead.'

'I haven't yet. I will, though, promise. I'm surprised he didn't manage to work it out, you know. He does have the brain of an accountant.'

'None of us worked it out.'

'Me and Marty were convinced that someone would. Fuckin' hell people are stupid.' Arthur started to laugh again.

'So, the big question, was it art then, mate?'

'It was whatever you want it to be. I'd definitely call it a performance. Entertainment, I suppose. If you want it to be art, then it was art. I am an artist after all.'

'Yeah, a fucking piss artist.' They both laughed. Johnny realised it was not the time for a deep analysis of what had taken place. There would be repercussions, but for the moment he would let Arthur revel in what he had pulled off.

***

Mark looked at Arthur as he spoke, his wild, dark hair, the slightly mad look in his eyes, his face flushed with intensity. It was this intensity that had first attracted him; that and the way that Arthur had been able to open his eyes to the world around him. However, it came at a price. Arthur always gave the impression that he lived for his art, but Mark had concluded that Arthur lived for Arthur.

'So, they're desperate to try to do us for something. The authorities seem to be really pissed off. I think we made it look a bit too easy. Marty has had a letter from the police telling him that they're looking into doing him for faking a death certificate. They haven't tried it with me yet, but I wouldn't be surprised if they do. The police have interviewed the funeral directors as well, but they've done nothing wrong. They genuinely thought there was a dead body in the coffin.'

'I suppose the guy who helped you get into the coffin on the morning of the funeral might be in trouble.'

'He might have been, but the funeral directors aren't interested in pursuing him, and I think the police will have trouble getting anywhere on their own. Surprisingly, the vicar seems to have a sense of humour; he thinks it's quite funny and has no interest in helping the police cook up a prosecution.'

'What about the Italians? They must have the best case against you, as well as Marty and the paramedics.'

'Well, their attitude I think reflects the cultural differences in our two societies. The British Pavilion has reopened, so all my sculptures are being shown now. They're treating the faked death as performance art; they fuckin' loved it.'

'The hospital isn't doing anything about the paramedics?'

'They just see it as helping an artist perform. That's how it's being seen in Italy. There's no question of any criminality.'

'That does seem very broadminded.'

'I would call it open minded, Mark. Open to new ideas, open to being entertained. We're still too stuffy in this country. Look at the tabloids. Making a story out of how I treated my parents. Fuckin' arseholes. Nothing about the art, the artistic merit of the whole thing.'

'Well, your mum and dad were pretty upset.'

'I've spoken to them on the phone. They're fine with it.' Arthur drained his pint glass. 'Fancy another?' he asked Mark.

'Why not?'

He watched Arthur walk up to the bar at the Compton Arms, one of their old haunts. He had done a lot of thinking over the past few days. He had definitely fallen out of love with Arthur; his lack of empathy, his lack of consideration for other people's feelings, not just Mark's, had been present before the faked death, but Mark had ignored these aspects of his personality. What Mark had concentrated on was his charisma, his creativity, his fuck-off attitude to the world, all traits that Mark had never possessed himself and that he tended to be drawn to in other people. He had realised that Johnny was not dissimilar, another rebel, but Johnny possessed empathy, which balanced him out.

Arthur came back with the drinks. They sipped on their pints of bitter. Arthur had now reverted to his more naturally taciturn nature. Previously, Mark had found these companionable silences relaxing, but this was no longer the case. He now felt he had to fill the silences.

'So, what next?' he asked.

'I've got some new ideas. More performance-led. I need to have some down time before I start on them. Potter around the studio. Caroline thinks we should enjoy the moment for a little while, let what has happened sink in, then hit the world with another event.'

'That sounds like a good idea. Let the dust settle.'

'For a bit, yeah. But I'll need to get working on something again soon.'

Mark could not imagine Arthur letting much time pass before his next project began in earnest. He loved being the centre of attention, but, more than that, there was something inside him driving him on. He was relentless in his pursuit of his goals; the creation of new art would have to come at any cost. Mark felt like no more than a staging post in Arthur's quest; he knew that he was already moving past him and would not look back. He was still theoretically Arthur's business manager as well as his lover, but he understood that both these roles were in their death throes. He took another sip of his beer. There would not be an emotional scene with Arthur. He would just stop calling; he would simply move on to the next lover, the next manager, presumably Caroline, the next project, and that would be that. Right now Mark was quite happy to just let that happen.

***

A letter from Caroline Schmidt to Henri le Cerf, written in French, translated into English:

Cher Henri

As you know, I am not one for sentimentality when it comes to relationships. While I was disappointed by the feelings you expressed to me in London, I have no intention of trying to change your mind. Once a relationship is over, it is over. However, there are some loose ends to tie up. As you know I like everything in life to be well ordered.

1. Arthur Swale has asked me to manage his business affairs as well as being his chosen gallery to display his works. This means that neither you nor Mark Arnold will be paid a commission for any sales of his works.
2. It is inevitable that our paths will cross both in Geneva and in Paris. I expect you to greet me as you would any friend and make conversation in the normal way but never to mention our previous relationship or discuss the past unless prompted by me.
3. I know at heart you are a gentleman, so I probably do not need to bring this up, but I would like your assurance by return that you will never discuss our physical relationship with anyone.
4. I have separately sent a small package of your personal items that were left at my apartment in Geneva. I left a few things with you in Paris. I would appreciate it if you would forward them on to me.

Finally, out of courtesy, I just want to let you know that my relationship with Arthur Swale is likely to move beyond the purely professional. You probably already know that he and Mark are no longer together.

Warmest regards
Caroline Schmidt

Henri read and re-read the short letter a few times. It was typically emotionless and, if anything, he felt relieved that he had written confirmation that the relationship was over. There was one glaring contradiction, though; the last thing someone desirous of a well-ordered life should do is have a relationship with Arthur Swale. Go figure that one out.

***

Sophie saw the familiar French number come up on her Nokia as it started to sound its ring. Johnny was back on tour and Amy was asleep upstairs, so she was free to talk. Juste knew that late in the evening was the best time to call if she wanted to chat.

'Comment ça va, ma puce?'

'I'm good, thanks. Back to normal, I think.'

'What is normal?'

'Well, you know what I mean.'

'How are you and Véronique?'

'Arguing like crazy. I just left the apartment to get away from the bitch.' Sophie thought she could hear the noise of a bar in the background. 'When I think about you, it makes me argue with her.'

'I'm sorry to hear that, but I know what you mean. Fortunately, Johnny's not here to argue with.'

'I wanted to tell you, I saw Henri the other night. He and Caroline have split. Did you know?'

'I knew it was likely to happen.'

'He didn't really want to talk much about it, but I think the whole faked-death débâcle was at the root of it. She knew what was happening from the beginning apparently and said nothing to Henri.'

'I don't think that was the only problem between them.'

'I can imagine. Beautiful, but she has a *froideur*.'

'I agree.'

'Unlike you, who has a *chaleur*.'

'Why thank you.'

'When shall we meet again?'

'I'll try to come to Paris again soon.'

'Yes, make it soon.'

'I'll do my best.'

'I have to go. Someone wants to talk to me. Urgently apparently.' There was some female laughter in the background. '*Amuse-toi bien, ma puce.*'

'You, too. *Bisous.*'

Juste had already gone. It sounded like she would be amusing herself more than Sophie tonight. It was good to talk to Juste from time to time, but she realised that, while Juste found her amusing and attractive, she was probably not much more than another notch on her bedpost. As luck would have it, she realised she had not fallen for Juste; it had not been much more than a crush. Sophie would add Juste to the names in her tent (rather than bedpost). She might never sleep with her again, and that would be fine, but she hoped they would be friends for life.

***

'I know you warned me, Mum, but I hope you understand why I had to get in touch with him.'

'It's taken me a while to come to terms with it, but, yes, I do understand. Like it or not, he's your dad. He's useless, but he is still your dad.'

'Useless at being a dad, but he's not useless, just very selfish. He seems incapable of considering other people's feelings.'

'Tell me something I don't know.' Mary Jones sipped at her mug of tea. He smiled at her, and she smiled back, her bright-blue eyes full of love. He was glad that they were back on speaking terms, bonding over Marty's uselessness.

'He did do a good job arranging Arthur's faked death.'

'Well, he had experience in that area, didn't he? It was as if he faked his own death after you were born.' They both chuckled.

'At least you can laugh about it now, Mum. You never even spoke about him for thirty years.'

'Not to you, but I used to moan about him to your gran from time to time.'

'Do you want to meet him?'

'No I do not. Not on your Nelly.'

They laughed again.

'I'm having a bit of a break from him, as a matter of fact. I realised that I saw a bit too much of him a bit too quickly. He's a bit all-or-nothing, Marty.'

'Tell me about it.'

'Either he can't see enough of you, or he doesn't see you at all. I don't think he even realises I'm having a break from him. He's drifted away anyway.'

'How's Amy?'

'She's great.'

'And Sophie?'

'Also great. I think. Coming back from the tour every couple of weeks really helps us all. I think we would be in danger of drifting apart if I wasn't doing that.'

'And are you staying off the booze, and that other rubbish?'

'All things in moderation, Mum. I'm still drinking, but I'm controlling it rather than it controlling me.'

'Glad to hear it – but you be careful.'

'I will be careful. We're going up to London tonight to meet up with Mark and Henri. A reunion of sorts. Sophie's mum is looking after Amy. We're getting the last train home.'

'That'll be nice.'

'Yes, kind of a normal night out in all the madness.'

'You need a bit more normal, Johnny.'

'Yes, maybe I do.'

***

Henri seemed to have regained his usual confidence and composure.

'We'll have a bottle of the *premier cru* Chablis with the oysters and a bottle of the Puligny-Montrachet with the John Dory fillets.'

The four friends always seemed to leave it to Henri to order the wine – he was French, after all. He was wearing a white open-necked cotton shirt, under what Sophie thought might be a Gucci suit. It was of a lightweight grey wool with a slight sheen to it; a little *Goodfellas* but in a sophisticated way. Sophie approved; it reminded her why she had fallen for his charm in the first place. She wondered momentarily if she would again.

'You flash bastard.'

'What is it you English say? If you've got it, flaunt it. Well, I am flaunting it.'

Johnny laughed, and even Mark smiled. Johnny was wearing his hair a little shorter at the moment, still quite messy, but he, too, looked good. He'd picked up a tan through the summer, and he looked sun kissed and healthy. He was wearing a new baggy leather jacket and had taken to baggy jeans and a low belt; it was a kind of hip-hop meets Britpop look that suited him. Mark was quiet, Sophie thought. She guessed he was still not over the whole Arthur thing. She wondered if he knew about Arthur and Caroline. If he didn't, he probably would by the end of the evening.

'I assume you all remember the last time that we were here?' she asked them all.

'At Quaglino's? It was after *Sensation*, wasn't it?' Mark responded first.

'Of course,' said Henri. 'That was the day I met the shark. It changed me for ever.' He said it with a smile, and they all laughed. He continued, 'I'm joking, but I suppose it did in a way. It opened my eyes to a world I knew little about. And look where that took me.'

'And me,' said Mark. 'That exhibition was responsible for at least two failed relationships that I know of. I take it you know that Arthur and Caroline now seem to be more than professionally acquainted.'

'That's a very polite way of saying that they're shagging,' Johnny said in such a way as to force both Mark and Henri to laugh.

In a way, thought Sophie, it was even responsible for the failure of another relationship, as it had indirectly led to the end of her affair with Henri. She caught his eye and wondered if he was thinking the same thing.

'You know, it's funny but I think that exhibition had a big effect on me, too. The Tracey Emin tent has really stayed in my mind. Not just the physical artwork, but the sentiment behind it, the way she opened herself up completely to the viewer. I don't know whether or not you remember, but it was called *Everyone I Have Ever Slept With*. Did any of you go into the tent?' The other three shook their heads. 'Well, I thought that it was just a list of lovers inside at first, but when you go and sit in it you realise it isn't; the names embroidered inside include friends, her twin brother, drinking buddies, even two aborted foetuses, as well as her lovers. I'd met her a few minutes before I sat in the tent, and it made me feel so close to her.' She stopped for a moment feeling herself well up. 'It seemed to open my eyes somehow, not just to pain and suffering but to love and the many forms it takes.

'Very deep, darling.' Johnny was obviously uncomfortable with what she was saying and tried to make a joke of it. The others stayed silent. The silence was broken by the arrival of the oysters.

'I wish I'd taken a proper look at that,' Mark said. 'Although I suspect my eyes were a little closed to its merit back then. My eyes were only on one thing: a man dressed in black with a northern accent.' Now they all laughed. Sophie watched discreetly as Henri messily despatched his first oyster. There was definitely still something there, she thought.

'You know, I must admit to having been a bit of a philistine when it came to art before I met Arthur. He really opened my eyes. He stood me in front of that Chapman Brothers sculpture with the unpronounceable title, you know the one which looks like it's made of adolescent shop mannequins. I had no idea what to think of it, but, as he talked, I noticed more and more about it. The humour, a satirical element, the misplaced genitals; a feeling of child abuse or exploitation or something unpleasant. He made me look properly at the work. He also kind of granted me the freedom to tell him what I thought of it without judging me. That was a very attractive feature of his, particularly at the beginning.' Mark stopped and sipped on his Chablis. He had surprised Sophie; he was not normally that unguarded. Arthur must really have done him some good.

Then Johnny spoke. 'I think I told you after the exhibition, but I was very struck by another piece, *Dead Dad*.'

'Yes, I remember you talking about that,' said Mark.

'Oh my God. It was Marty, wasn't it? I remember now, you talked about it the last time we were here. A kind of real-life sculpture of a naked, dead old man.' Sophie had joined up the dots.

'That's the one. It was the prompt I needed to go and find my father. I'm not sure that it was a good idea, but at least I found him.' This raised another round of sniggering.

'And where is he now?' asked Henri.

'We're having a break, not that Marty realises. He's a bit too self-absorbed for that.'

'You got a hit song out of it, too,' said Mark.

'Yes, I suppose I did.' Johnny's voice trailed off.

'Without Marty maybe there would have been no faked death,' said Henri.

'No, maybe not, although I'm pretty sure it was Arthur's idea.'

Sophie noticed that Mark was looking at Johnny affectionately, aware of his vulnerability. In the past the look would have made her jealous, but it no longer had that effect on her.

'But was it art?' she asked.

'Was what art?' Henri asked.

'The faked death.'

'Isn't art a bit like religion,' said Johnny, 'a little bit death obsessed?'

'Have you been listening to Damien Hirst?' asked Henri. 'The shark, of course, is all about death. Not only is it dead but it's also a celebration of it being dead.'

'But Arthur wasn't dead,' said Mark. 'There was no beauty in what he did. It was just deception, surely.'

'I'm not sure,' said Sophie. 'Don't you think that things are often not what they seem in art? People often misinterpret or misconstrue a work of art. In a way, Arthur just took that misconception or that ability to misconstrue to an extreme conclusion. What appeared to be his own death was in fact a fake.'

At that moment the fish and the white burgundy arrived, and everyone's attention turned to them before Sophie had an answer. She had been wrestling with this question since the funeral, and now that she had had the opportunity to articulate her thoughts she was in no doubt. Arthur had been deceitful, he had tricked his audience, perhaps more than any artist before him, but, of course, it had been art. Not deceit, not even artfulness, it had been art.

And it had also been art that had brought them back together, the four of them, inextricably linked to one another. First it had been poker, and now it was art that was their common bond. She looked at the three boys and realised she would not have it any other way.

By the same author

Instinct or Intuition?

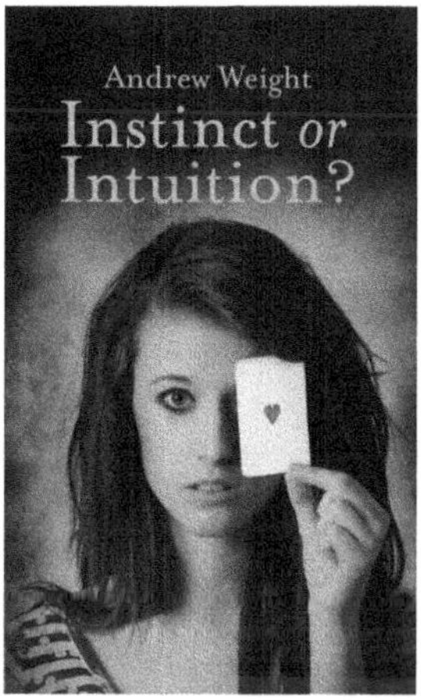

Before *Artfulness or Deceit?* there was *Instinct or Intuition?* It's 1989, and Sophie Arlington's life is about to change for good. She's just met aspiring musician Johnny Jones over a hand of poker, and she's so drawn to his high cheekbones that she ends up inviting him into her bed. Also at the same poker table are Mark Arnold, Sophie's old friend and flatmate, and the predatory but charming Henri le Cerf, a French-Swiss soon-to-be private banker.

The four friends meet over the next few years in London, Rye, Paris and Lausanne to play poker, to do business and to make love. But their lives become more entwined than any of them could have imagined, as the bluff of the poker table is overshadowed by the deceit at the heart of their relationships.

£9.99

PAPERBACK ISBN 978-0-9927568-0-2 / EPUB ISBN 978-0-9927568-1-9 / MOBIPOCKET ISBN 978-0-9927568-2-6 / PDF ISBN 978-0-9927568-3-3

Milton Keynes UK
Ingram Content Group UK Ltd.
UKHW050603110324
438959UK00022B/494

9 780992 756840